COMPREHENSIVE RESEARCH
AND STUDY GUIDE

Allen Tate

BLOOM'S
MAJOR
POETS

EDITED AND WITH AN INTRODUCTION
BY HAROLD BLOOM

CURRENTLY AVAILABLE

BLOOM'S MAJOR POETS

Maya Angelou
John Ashbery
Elizabeth Bishop
William Blake
Gwendolyn Brooks
Robert Browning
Geoffrey Chaucer
Sameul Taylor Coleridge
Hart Crane
E.E. Cummings
Dante
Emily Dickinson
John Donne
H.D.
Thomas Hardy
Seamus Heaney
A.E. Housman
T. S. Eliot
Robert Frost
Seamus Heaney
Homer
Langston Hughes
John Keats
W.S. Merwin
John Milton
Marianne Moore
Sylvia Plath
Edgar Allan Poe
Poets of World War I
Christina Rossetti
Wallace Stevens
Mark Strand
Shakespeare's Poems & Sonnets
Percy Shelley
Allen Tate
Alfred, Lord Tennyson
Walt Whitman
William Carlos Williams
William Wordsworth
William Butler Yeats

COMPREHENSIVE RESEARCH AND STUDY GUIDE

Allen Tate

CHELSEA HOUSE PUBLISHERS
A Haights Cross Communications Company
Philadelphia

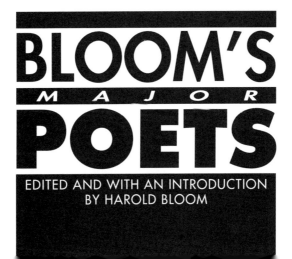

BLOOM'S MAJOR POETS

EDITED AND WITH AN INTRODUCTION BY HAROLD BLOOM

A Haights Cross Communications Company

Printed and bound in the United States of America.

First Printing
1 3 5 7 9 8 6 4 2

Library of Congress Cataloging-in-Publication Data

Allen Tate / [edited by] Harold Bloom.
p. cm. — (Bloom's major poets)
Includes bibliographical references and index.
ISBN 0-7910-7889-2
1. Tate, Allen, 1899—-Criticism and interpretation. I. Bloom, Harold. II. Series.
PS3539.A74Z56 2004
818'.5209—dc22

2004002632

Contributing Editor: Gabriel Welsch

Cover design by Keith Trego

Layout by EJB Publishing Services

CONTENTS

User's Guide 7

About the Editor 8

Editor's Note 9

Introduction 10

Biography of Allen Tate 12

Critical Analysis of "Ode to the Confederate Dead" 18

Critical Views on "Ode to the Confederate Dead" 25

- George Hemphill on the Poem's Formative Aspects 25
- Ferman Bishop on Tate's Revision Process 29
- Radcliffe Squires Explicates the Poem 39
- Robert S. Dupree on Tate's Parody of Religious Ideals 47
- William Doreski on the Context of Tate's Voice 53
- Langdon Hammer on the Presence of Other Modernists 55

Critical Analysis of "The Mediterranean" 63

Critical Views on "The Mediterranean" 66

- George Hemphill onTate's Characteristic Tension 66
- Radcliffe Squires on Tate's Intellectual "Home" 68
- Robert S. Dupree on the Poem's Suggestive Language 71
- William Doreski on Tate's Connection to Baudelaire 75

Critical Analysis of "Aeneas at Washington" 78

Critical Views on "Aeneas at Washington" 82

- Radcliffe Squires on Tate's Pairs of Poems 82
- Robert S. Dupree on the Poem's Imaginative Leap 84
- Elsa Nettels on the Poem's Agrarian Statement 88

Critical Analysis of "The Swimmers" 92

Critical Views on "The Swimmers" 96

- Radcliffe Squires on Tate's Formal Approach 96
- Robert S. Dupree on the Poem's Narrative and Symbolism 97
- William Doreski on Tate's Breaking New Ground 102
- Thomas A. Underwood on Tate's Social Thinking 106

Works by Allen Tate 113
Works about Allen Tate 116
Acknowledgments 121
Index of Themes and Ideas 122

USER'S GUIDE

This volume is designed to present biographical, critical, and bibliographical information on the author and the author's best-known or most important poems. Following Harold Bloom's editor's note and introduction is a concise biography of the author that discusses major life events and important literary accomplishments. A critical analysis of each poem follows, tracing significant themes, patterns, and motifs in the work. As with any study guide, it is recommended that the reader read the poem beforehand and have a copy of the poem being discussed available for quick reference.

A selection of critical extracts, derived from previously published material, follows each thematic analysis. In most cases, these extracts represent the best analysis available from a number of leading critics. Because these extracts are derived from previously published material, they will include the original notations and references when available. Each extract is cited, and readers are encouraged to check the original publication as they continue their research. A bibliography of the author's writings, a list of additional books and articles on the author and their work, and an index of themes and ideas conclude the volume.

ABOUT THE EDITOR

Harold Bloom is Sterling Professor of the Humanities at Yale University. He is the author of over 20 books, and the editor of more than 30 anthologies of literary criticism.

Professor Bloom's works include *Shelley's Mythmaking* (1959), *The Visionary Company* (1961), *Blake's Apocalypse* (1963), *Yeats* (1970), *A Map of Misreading* (1975), *Kabbalah and Criticism* (1975), *Agon: Toward a Theory of Revisionism* (1982), *The American Religion* (1992), *The Western Canon* (1994), and *Omens of Millennium: The Gnosis of Angels, Dreams, and Resurrection* (1996). *The Anxiety of Influence* (1973) sets forth Professor Bloom's provocative theory of the literary relationships between the great writers and their predecessors. His most recent books include *Shakespeare: The Invention of the Human*, a 1998 National Book Award finalist, *How to Read and Why* (2000), *Stories and Poems for Extremely Intelligent Children of All Ages* (2001), *Genius: A Mosaic of One Hundred Exemplary Creative Minds* (2002), and *Hamlet: Poem Unlimited* (2003).

Professor Bloom earned his Ph.D. from Yale University in 1955 and has served on the Yale faculty since then. He is a 1985 MacArthur Foundation Award recipient and served as the Charles Eliot Norton Professor of Poetry at Harvard University in 1987–88. In 1999 he was awarded the prestigious American Academy of Arts and Letters Gold Medal for Criticism. Professor Bloom is the editor of several other Chelsea House series in literary criticism, including BLOOM'S MAJOR SHORT STORY WRITERS, BLOOM'S MAJOR NOVELISTS, BLOOM'S MAJOR DRAMATISTS, BLOOM'S MODERN CRITICAL INTERPRETATIONS, BLOOM'S MODERN CRITICAL VIEWS, BLOOM'S BIOCRITIQUES, BLOOM'S GUIDES, BLOOM'S MAJOR LITERARY CHARACTERS, and BLOOM'S PERIOD STUDIES.

EDITOR'S NOTE

My Introduction contrasts "The Mediterranean," a poem that shows Allen Tate's affinity with Hart Crane, to "Aeneas at Washington," where the idiom of T.S. Eliot is dominant.

All six of the critical analyses of "Ode to the Confederate Dead" seem to me useful, but I am particularly helped by Langdon Hammer's acute perceptions. Hammer shrewdly notes Tate's recapitulation of his identification with Eliot and repudiation of Hart Crane. He captures the irony of Crane's continued presence in the poem's metric and cognitive music.

"The Mediterranean" receives four erudite commentaries here, emphasizing Tate's evocations of Vergil and Baudelaire, useful supplements to the surmise in my Introduction that Hart Crane's ghost also hovers in this poem.

"Aeneas at Washington," far more Eliotic than Vergilian, is seen by three critics here as an exemplification of Tate's "fierce Latinity."

"The Swimmers," probably Tate's most socially problematical poem, is illuminated by four approaches here, all of which suggest that this work's creation could not resolve the blockage of Tate's imaginative vision.

INTRODUCTION

Harold Bloom

I met Allen Tate only twice, and was moved by the poignance of his memories of Hart Crane, his exact contemporary and close friend. Tate's literary criticism was very much in the mode of T.S. Eliot, and I always greatly preferred Tate's own poetry to his work as a critic. Northrop Frye, reviewing Tate's collected essays, found in them what Frye called the Eliotic myth of the Great Western Butterslide, in which a grand slab of classical, Catholic, and royalist butter slides down the centuries and melts, until it congeals again in Eliot's *The Waste Land*.

Though a resolute New Critic, in Eliot's wake, Tate ultimately was as much a late Romantic poet as Eliot proved to be. Though Tate increasingly repudiated Hart Crane's *The Bridge* while hailing Eliot's *The Waste Land*, the idiom of Crane never abandoned the would-be classicist. Crane's pentameter quatrains easily can be mistaken for Tate's while Eliot's fascinating blend of Tennyson and Whitman (his true precursors) yielded a very different mode.

Tate's "Ode to the Confederate Dead" strives to be Eliotic, yet the voice of Hart Crane keeps breaking in:

> The brute curiosity of an angel's stare
> Turns you, like them, to stone,
> Transforms the heaving air
> Till plunged to a heavier world below
> You shift your sea-space blindly
> Heaving, turning like the blind crab.
>
> Dazed by the wind, only the wind
> The leaves flying, plunge

This would be at home anywhere in Crane's first volume, *White Buildings*. Even closer to Crane are the majestic quatrains that conclude "The Mediterranean," to me Tate's best poem:

Let us lie down once more by the breathing side
Of Ocean, where our live forefathers sleep
As if the Known Sea still were a month wide—
Atlantic howls but is no longer steep!

What country shall we conquer, what fair land
Unman our conquest and locate our blood
We've cracked the hemispheres with careless hand!
Now, from the Gates of Hercules we flood

Westward, westward till the barbarous brine
Whelms us to the tired land where tasseling corn,
Fat beans, grapes sweeter than muscadine
Rot on the vine: in that land were we born.

Tate is a permanent poet, though not of the eminence either of Eliot or of Hart Crane. The savage energy of "Aeneas at Washington" is Tate's own, even if the elegiac splendor of "The Mediterranean" always returns me to the somber and stately quatrains that conclude the canto of *The Bridge* titled "The River."

BIOGRAPHY OF

Allen Tate

In a recent essay in *The New Criterion*, critic David Yezzi summarized and, to a point, re-introduced, Allen Tate with the following paragraph:

> "Allen Tate displayed all the romantic qualities of a great artist: intellectual precocity, heavy drinking, prodigious libido, volatility in friendship, difficult views, and enough self-interest to bind the lot together. What he lacked was great art. Or so ran current estimates of Tate's career as a poet, critic, and man of letters, which spanned some sixty years, up to his death in 1979."

Only recently have critics and poets alike taken to reconsidering Tate and some other mid-century figures of Modernism and the New Criticism, and Yezzi's article displays the framework which makes reconsideration possible and useful. After his mock-salacious opener, Yezzi goes on to describe the three lives most poets have—their literary life, or the work itself; their actual biography; and finally, the life of their influence, the ways in which their words and ideas continue a life at large. While Yezzi points out that influence does not alone justify the enduring consideration of an individual's literary work, Tate presents as compelling a case for it as any writer.

John Orley Allen Tate was born in 1899 in Winchester, Kentucky, to parents John Orley Tate and Eleanor Parke Custis Varnell. His childhood was marked by disruption and frequent relocation because of his father's business. The business took its toll on the family, and the Tates were divorced in 1911. His two older brothers had already left the family, and so Allen moved with his mother. Finally, in 1918, he started at Vanderbilt University.

Despite divorce and the several moves, Tate's homeland did make a lasting impression on the boy, though after leaving for Vanderbilt University, he never returned for any long periods. Even his bout with tuberculosis failed to send him back; he spent time in the mountains of North Carolina recovering. Tate's memory of the place and his constant preoccupation with it in his work led him towards writers of similar concern. Thus, Tate is now most often recalled as part of the Southern Literary Renaissance, an elder statesman to younger writers like Flannery O'Connor and Walker Percy, and a fellow traveler with such luminaries as William Faulkner, Robert Penn Warren, and John Crowe Ransom.

At Vanderbilt, Tate became associated with a group known as the Fugitives, a group whose members included John Crowe Ransom and Robert Penn Warren. The Fugitives was essentially a group of poets and other intellectuals who discussed philosophy and writing and sought out and supported the avante garde (though, according to George Hemphill, were bitterly divided over Eliot's *The Waste Land.*). Tate was the first undergraduate ever to be invited to join the group, an invitation extended by Ransom who, at the time, was an assistant professor of English at Vanderbilt, and Tate's teacher. The second undergraduate to receive an invitation was Tate's roommate at Vanderbilt, Robert Penn Warren.

The group, the Fugitives was presided over by a corpulent and widely erudite writer and scholar, Sidney Mttron Hirsch. The members would bring poems to read and discuss, occasionally arguing larger philosophical issues. According to Radcliffe Squires' account, two "passionate warriors" polarized the debate on poetry: "[Donald] Davidson arguing for a regional poetry, not, of course, just of the South, though he gladly supported that, but of a somewhat romantic apperception of an heroic past; and Tate arguing for an internationalism based on regionalism." Hirsch himself simply held that a system of symbolism and concepts underlaid all of the work of the Western tradition. The result of the meetings was, eventually, the push to establish a magazine, which they decided to call *The Fugitive*, a name derived from one of Hirsch's poems, and from a sense that their arguments and ideas regarding poetry were of just such a nefarious difference. The Fugitives came to be known as a group because of the magazine.

Of the Fugitives, Tate continued correspondence mostly with Robert Penn Warren, though they would eventually come to differences over political issues in the 1960s, particularly civil rights legislation. He also maintained a lifetime, though less frequent, epistolary conversation with Davidson. Those letters were collected and published in 1974.

After leaving Vanderbilt, Tate taught high school for a year in West Virginia before traveling further. In 1924, Tate went to New York where his new friend Hart Crane introduced him to Malcolm Cowley, Kenneth Burke, Slater Brown, and other literary figures. The same year, as a guest of Robert Penn Warren's back in Kentucky, Tate met Carolyn Gordon, whom he would eventually marry. Their daughter, Nancy, was born in 1925 and was quickly sent to live, for three years, with grandparents. By the winter of the same year, the Tates moved from Greenwich Village to Patterson, New Jersey (also the home of poet William Carlos Williams), and for a while, Hart Crane lived with them as well. According to several Tate scholars, Crane's presence in the house led to tension. He did not contribute much to the day-to-day tasks in the home, and Carolyn, reportedly, grew overly fond of him prior to his and Tate's agreement that he should find a new place to live. During the twenties, Tate lived as a freelance writer, penning reviews and articles for such places as *The Nation* and *The New Republic.* His wife, Caroline, provided the main financial support, working for the writer Ford Maddox Ford.

In 1929, Ford Maddox Ford helped Tate win a Guggenheim Fellowship, with which the Tates lived in London and Paris for the year. During their time their, Allen Tate came to know the members of the so-called Lost Generation: Ernest Hemingway, F. Scott Fitzgerald, Harry and Caresse Crosby, Gertrude Stein, and others. While the time spent in Paris provided Tate with even more resolve regarding the reinvention of literary forms, it also led him to revise some of his opinions regarding the content of literary art. In his early years with the Fugitives, Tate advocated the international and the cosmopolitan. But after working in Paris and living in New York, Tate began to rethink his position, especially as so much of his native region was celebrated and, to a large extent, eulogized in his work. In essence, travels abroad gave Tate the necessary distance from his homeland to begin to consider its heritage and value, as opposed to what he felt, as a younger man, was its stifling provincialism.

But even as he rejected older forms of literary art, he nonetheless embraced classical antiquity, American Catholicism, and so-called high culture. He did not so much reject structure altogether as replace one set of governance for another, one that, like many Modernists, he felt grew "organically" out of the culture of the time, preserving ineffable and timeless aspects of "classical" civilization and art. As a young man, Tate embraced the *avant garde* in literature, pursued it in the enclaves of Paris and New York, and wrote it himself. However, by the mid-1930s, Tate was questioning, and finding wanting, the morés, manners, and values of modernity. Together with many of his fellow writers from the Fugitives days, he was embroiled in and dedicating much of his effort to two ambitious projects of cultural architecture: the Southern Agrarian movement and the New Criticism.

Tate was one of many writers to appear in the 1930 anthology/manifesto *I'll Take My Stand*, a defense of the then-strengthening Agrarian movement. For Tate, Agrarianism was a means of saving the culture from the decline it experienced from the influences of industrialization, disillusionment, and moral decay. Tate was already being drawn toward Catholicism, and he saw the Agrarian south, with strong, local cultures based on agricultural economies and regional concern, as the only humane alternative to the destructive industrialism of the North. With some variations and developments, he believed in the philosophy for the rest of his life. The 1930s, thus, saw Tate produce a number of volumes of prose, mostly essays on poetry and ideas, but some novels as well. It was also in 1937 that Tate began his lifelong friendship and mentorship with the poet Robert Lowell.

Tate was also one of several writers involved and named in John Crowe Ransom's enormously influential book, *The New Criticism*, published in 1941. The New Criticism sought to treat literary work as a sacrosanct source, and the only means of its own interpretation, introducing the world to the notion of the "close reading." Only by reading the text, and nothing but the text, could one derive any real meaning. It, too, was a sort of regionalism to which Tate could ally his efforts.

Through the 1940s, with a family to support and his star still on the rise, Tate took to making money. He was a peripatetic teacher, working at a variety of institutions for short periods, never fully embracing the life of the professional academic until his earning a professorial position at the University of Minnesota in 1951. (He would hold the position until his retirement, in 1968). Overall, he taught for brief periods at Princeton, New York University, the University of Chicago, Oxford, and Rome. Tate converted to Catholicism in 1950, after a two-decade search for a faith more intellectually consistent with his work and personally satisfying than "the culturally dominant evangelical Protestantism of his geographic region," according to Peter Huff.

After years of stormy relations (Tate and Gordon divorced and remarried in 1946) and Tate's legendary womanizing, the couple separated in 1955 and divorced for good in 1959. The same year, Tate married poet Isabella Gardner; the marriage would not last. Carolyn Gordon, whom Gale H. Carrithers characterized in the *Southern Review* as "wronged and ferocious" went on to publish her novels *The Strange Children* (1951) and *The Malefactors* (1956), which nastily detail their life together. Though teaching then at Minnesota, Tate continued to lecture and travel around the United States and the world, to keep up his role as Catholic intellectual, literary luminary and, increasingly, elder statesman. He had already won the National Institute of Arts and Letters Award in 1948, and in 1956 he won the coveted Bollingen Prize for poetry. He was also, slowly, coming to realize some of the problems with his Agrarian friends and their ideas regarding the growing civil rights movement. Thomas Underwood's work outlines Tate's thinking and changes over these years.

In 1963, Tate won the Academy of American Poets award and, in 1964 in Minneapolis, he met Helen Heinz, who would become his third wife, and who would nurse him through the last several years of his life. By the 1970s, his place in American culture and literature seemingly secure (he could not, from his position, then foresee the great changes to come in literary scholarship and reputation-making), he was ever more weakened by emphysema. He was invited to Princeton University to give a series of lectures in 1973, and collapsed during one. As the awards came in—the Oscar Williams award, Mark Rothko award, Ingram Merrill award, and National Medal for Literature, all in 1976—his physical strength ebbed. A group of his admirers, including Malcolm Cowley and Howard Nemerov, attempted to lobby Stockholm to earn Tate the Nobel Prize. It was the one award he did not win. In failing health, he returned to Nashville by the mid-seventies and, in 1979, at the age of 80, Allen Tate died.

CRITICAL ANALYSIS OF

"Ode to the Confederate Dead"

"Ode to the Confederate Dead" is Tate's most famous and most often discussed poem. Some critics have pointed out that its very title probably contributed most forcefully to the decline in Tate's readership and currency among literary critics writing after the mid-sixties; the notion of an ode to dead soldiers was seen by many, incorrectly, as an ode to the confederacy itself and the horrific crimes of slavery, Jim Crow, and the like. However, Tate's poem is far more about memory and loss, the trials of modernity, and the impassive march of forgetting than it is about any lionizing of the South.

That's not to say there is *no* celebration of a past. But as several scholars have pointed out, the South for which Tate pens elegies and odes is an ideal that never existed, and a ghost of an idea that Tate and other Agrarians thought could *yet* exist, specifically as an antidote to the grinding destruction of industrialism. Industrialism, they thought, was a scourge uniquely of the North, despite assertions by historians, including C. Vann Woodward, that the very industrial society so demonized by Tate and his contemporaries was the same society that brought the South back as an economically viable region, and which led to its current burgeoning.

The poem begins by locating the speaker in a cemetery, viewing the stones: "Row after row with strict impunity/ The headstones yield their names to the element". The speaker feels, then, the wrongness in the fading names, the fading memories. The stones cannot be punished, they do this with "strict impunity". The element itself is unfeeling, a wind that "whirrs without recollection" and so resembles the land, the people, among which the long-dead soldiers are buried. They are being forgotten, it is clear.

Even the leaves, evoked and moved in the next six lines, are complicit. The cover the ditches and sunken graves, they are a "casual sacrament," an observance of death, a "seasonal" reminder of its "eternity." The speaker feels that their movement is witnessed and even caused by a god somewhere, through "the fierce scrutiny/ Of heaven," and their noise is the meaning of mortality, a murmur reminding the speaker, again, of death. The evocation of religion and a deity is palpable in the first stanza, with the use of words including "sacrament," "heaven," and "eternity." As well, desolation is present, in the image of graves sunken to become "troughs," and the ever-fading names on the stones. The only noise is the leaves, their skitter a muted death rattle.

Yet, in the next stanza, the speaker notes that the graveyard, while desolate, is a place where "memories grow," and is perhaps why the speaker has returned to the place. He notes, too, that while the bodies are interred, they are "not/ Dead". (The line break underscores the dual meaning; the bodies are "not," and yet, on the next line, their nullification is clearly modified.) They feed the grass. They are fertilizer, a loaded image and idea in an agrarian culture, and an image somewhat familiar from Sandburg's "The Tombs," from over a decade before. On thinking of how the bodies, never gone, enrich the grass of the "thousand acres," the speaker exhorts, "Thing of the autumns that have come and gone!" He characterizes the autumn, November, as zealously wearing away at the stones, at memory itself, carrying on with the "humors of the year," to strain "the uncomfortable angels that rot/ On the slabs". The time and the month carry, the *current* time, work their inexorable damage on memory and the images of religion and honor that occupy the graveyard. Tate characterizes the modern passage of time just as he would the condition of modernity itself.

The gaze of the angels staring out, the speaker assures the reader, "Turns you, like them, to stone," and in so doing, takes you into the "heavier world below," a Hades, perhaps, or an ocean, since the following image is that of the skittering blind crab, moved, just as the leaves, by forces both divine and uncontrollable. Just as the wind is moved by "the fierce scrutiny of heaven," so is the "crab" moved by the "brute curiosity" of an angel's stare, and the "sea-space" of a netherworld, or death.

The next stanza, a mere two lines, is the first of a total of four such couplets which specifically single out images related to the leaves. The leaves evolve a role in the poem, but here they start "Dazed by the wind, only the wind," before we learn they are flying, and that they plunge. The leaves, propelled (as told in the first stanza) by some divine force, are stunned, as if the wind is sudden, a cold brush.

The couplet provides a shift in the poem as well, as the speaker moves to consider then, with the reader, "who [has] waited by the wall" to the graveyard. This monologue addresses a specific idealized individual. Some (Bishop, for one—see below) have suggested that the speaker addresses Tiresias, the Theban seer, who has the ability to navigate the underworld and advise others who wish to go there. At the same time, given Tate's connections to the region and his thoughts about it, it is as likely a specific address as it is a universal one. The address reminds the reader how much he or she knows about what led to the fate of the bodies interred within the wall.

The speaker reminds the reader of the war, something they both remember. With the possibility of Tiresias being the addressee, the parallels between the Trojan War and the Civil War are reasserted, as they often are in Tate's work. The terms of what is remembered are contradictory, apocalyptic, and instinctive: "the twilight certainty of an animal" has overtones of the kill, the pursuit, and the hunt. "Those midnight restitutions of the blood" speaks to sacrifice, to corporeal honor and thickness, to payment in flesh. War's specific landscapes are evoked: "the immitigable pines, the smoky frieze of the sky, the sudden call": all evocations of the battlefield, the charge, the unyielding landscape that consumes them even now. The bodies are a "cold pool left by the mounting flood," and the notion of a world comprised of one substance, a philosophical oneness, is "muted" by the experience of defeat, of division and difference.

Zeno and Parmenides are evoked as metaphysicians who viewed the universe and world as consisting of a single substance, constitutive of reality. Tate's use of them here as muted evokes the sense, in a classical manner, that those on the losing side of the battle, those living in the era of Reconstruction, might have found such a notion improbable, distant as they felt from the new industrial and political realities of the South.

The most conspicuous contradictions come in the last seven lines of the stanza, when the speaker reminds the reader of the "unimportant shrift of death"—a contrast against the importance death and mortality have been given in the monologue so far. The use of "shrift," now uncommon in typical speech, refers to penance and absolution. Shrift thus again conflates death and the divine. In this case, the penance due for a life of sin—death and consequent afterlife, upon absolution—is unimportant to what is left. And the reasons for death, the "vision" and "arrogant circumstance," are praised, as the cause is praised, that which caused men to simply react, to hurry "beyond decision." But it is bitter praise of a system that "*should* be yours tomorrow" (emphasis mine) but will never be. According to George Hemphill, Hart Crane pointed out to Tate that what this section of the poem decried is the excess of chivalry, the unnecessary praise of arrogance and valor that led to so much death and, ultimately, loss of region, spirit, identity (see the Hemphill excerpt below).

Then, for the second time, the image of the leaves stops the speaker. He only sees them, doesn't hear them, and this time, as he sees them, they "expire." They are already dead, of course, falling from the tree. Just as the bodies in the ground are already dead, and yet Tate's speaker implies they are not dead until, perhaps, their memory falls as well. In this way, the leaf is a correlative. It is not truly dead until it plunges and hits the ground, to then rot.

In the next stanza, Tate's speaker asks the reader to "Turn your eyes to the immoderate past," to remember the hazy soldiers, indeterminate in their presence, hellish even, as "Demons," and in spite of terrifying presence, "they will not last." The next lines are a litany of battles, only one of which the Confederate forces won, and even it, at Bull Run, was a limited victory that led to subsequently doomed campaign of invasion. Tate's speaker says to the reader, "Lost in that orient of the thick-and-fast [the tumult of battle and the images of past confrontations]/ You will curse the setting sun."

The leaves come in then, for the third time, but in this instance, building on the image concluding of the previous stanza. "Cursing only the leaves crying/ Like an old man in a storm", with the play of the enjambment signaling the lines' two possible meanings. Either the man is crying, or the sound of the leaves is like a crying. The sound segues into a reverie, wherein the speaker says the reader hears "the shout" and "the crazy hemlocks point/ With troubled fingers to the silence which/ Smothers you, a mummy, in time." Thus, just as earth covers the body, the land points to a horrible quiet which envelopes the reader, whom Tate's speakers likes to a mummy, another version of a corpse. The soldiers are buried by earth, the reader (and, perhaps, the speaker) are buried by the silence which, like the headstones, yields the soldiers and their society to oblivion. And while the speaker and the reader hear all of this, the hound, an icon for Tate's remembered South, perhaps hears only wind, and none of what it says. The hound, unlike the jaguar which follows, is not actively hunting, is not predatory, in the way other figures in the poem are.

The following stanza poses the essential question of the poem—what to do when ceremony, tradition, and all their trappings fail us? What to do when life seems disconnected to faith and living, when determinism tramples our best efforts at self-determinism? Now that the bodies of the soldiers are so part of the soil that "their blood/ Stiffens the saltier oblivion of the seas"—that is, now that they are so disparate as to be part of the great waters of the earth—now that they are so gone, "What shall we who count our days ... with a commemorial woe ... say of the bones, unclean/ Whose verdurous anonymity will grow?" The speaker asks of the lush field, the "insane green" that is now all that is left of once chivalrous men, what can we say, we who have failed to feel their presence and have made of them, like the leaves, scarcely a murmur? As the adjectives pile up—grim, lean, insane, furious—and match with such benign images as the verdurous, the "lyric" which "seeds the mind," and the genteel notion of chivalry, the great conflict shows itself. We will forget, eventually, despite any effort. Life goes on, to put it colloquially. The world is unforgiving in its passage, in its urge to wholeness. The final couplet on the leaves states, "We shall say only the leaves/ Flying, plunge and expire"—and they will blindly insist that only leaves—and not men—die.

The penultimate stanza continues, noting again that "We shall only say the leaves whispering/ In the improbable mist of nightfall/ That flies on multiple wing". The stanza describes how night is the only permanence, death as the condition from which, for a brief moment, we are liberated to life. It is "the beginning and the end," and life is simply "mute speculation, the patient curse/ That stones the eyes, or like the jaguar leaps/ For his own image in a jungle pool, his victim." The repetition of "pool" calls to mind, again, the presence of Zeno and Parmenides, in the fourth stanza. The pool is the complete universe, the one matter of which everything is a part. Thus, the jaguar leaps at his reflection, fooled into thinking it is separate from the whole. The pool and the reflection also calls up the myth of Narcissus, and the vanity of self regard. If the metaphysicians are right—and Tate's speaker acts as if they are—then life's mute speculation on difference and individuality is a "patient curse" that fools us into believing we are somehow independent of the universe, and not set on a course to return to our former state.

"What shall we say who have knowledge/ Carried to the heart? Shall we take the act/ To the grave? Shall we, more hopeful, set up the grave/ In the house? The ravenous grave?" The final lines of the stanza are a heap of paradoxes, all asking on the failure of something, be it belief, a system, or a cause. The fatalism of the last two lines, in particular, is of the sort that Thomas Hardy may have, throwing up his hands in the face of an overwhelming cosmic reality. But Tate's particular questions acknowledge the eventuality of death, regardless of what fails. If we are more hopeful, strangely, we put the grave in the house, to shorten the trip, so to speak.

But even for this speaker, such fatalism has to come to an end. He says, "Leave now/ The shut gate and the decomposing wall" and do not bother the fading memory, stories, names, lives. The serpent—an image of evil and temptation, here presented as gentle, and thus the more insidious, lurking in the mulberry bush, a plant of children's songs and graveyards—makes noise within: "Riots with his tongue through the hush—/ Sentinel of the grave who counts us all." Even if the "serpent" is a mere silkworm, the treatment here expands its significance into something more sinister, with, perhaps, a suitably industrious base from which the poet expands. The image is the reminder that the yard will wait for all of us, that the anonymity that is descending upon the soldiers will await us as well. The resignation of belief and chivalry and woe and the rest of it is, as the serpent's vigil suggests, the fate that awaits all of us. As Crane pointed out to Tate, what passes is more than lives, but ways of life, and while the poem laments the loss, it also suggests its inevitability. The ode then is more than mere elegy; it is an ode to time passing, horrible as that may seem.

CRITICAL VIEWS ON

"Ode to the Confederate Dead"

GEORGE HEMPHILL ON THE POEM'S FORMATIVE ASPECTS

[George Hemphill is an Assistant Professor of English at the University of Connecticut. He is the editor of *Discussions of Poetry: Rhythm and Sound*. Here, Hemphill discusses some of Tate's social ideas as represented in the poem.]

The beginnings of the "Ode to the Confederate Dead" belong to this period. The very success of this poem in later years, the number of times it has been reprinted in anthologies, the notoriety Tate himself lent it with his essay "Narcissus as Narcissus" (1938)—these things have distorted the casual reader's notion of Tate. The title alone—and some readers recall little but titles—is cause of offense to many. Why "Ode"? Doesn't that mean public celebration? Let the dead bury their dead; no use picking old sores. That Tate would agree is not much help to those who won't bother to find out that he agrees.

The poem started out as an elegy and did not reach its final form until 1936. Early in January 1927 Tate sent copies of the first version to Ransom, Davidson, and Crane. The Princeton Library owns the earliest typescript, with Ransom's marginal comments. Davidson did not like the poetic direction his friend seemed to be taking: "Your 'Elegy,'" he said, "is not for the Confederate dead but for your own dead emotion." Crane made some extremely perceptive criticisms, and understood immediately what the poem was about: "Chivalry, a tradition of excess, active faith ... '*should* be yours tomorrow' but ... will not persist nor find any way into action."

That is, the "Ode to the Confederate Dead" has a lot in common with *The Great Gatsby*. The man at the gate of the Confederate graveyard has "knowledge carried to the heart" and Jay Gatsby has "some heightened sensitivity to the promises of life"; they come to the same thing. The man at the gate allows himself to imagine, if only for a moment, that the leaves he sees blown by the wind are charging infantry; Gatsby, when Nick Carraway tells him he can't repeat the past, says: "Can't repeat the past? Why of course you can." The man at the gate has "waited for the angry resolution / Of those desires that should be [his] tomorrow"; Gatsby "believed in the green light." Both men are accounted failures, or rather they fail and are memorialized in their failure. Neither is an international *Waste Land* character. The man at the gate is philosophical, like Hamlet, but he is not a prince; he is ineffectual, like Prufrock, but he is not ridiculous; he is as American as Jay Gatsby but he is not a vulgarian "in the service of a vast, vulgar, meretricious beauty." Poor Gatsby really did go to Oxford, but talks about it in such a way as to convince Nick Carraway he is lying; somewhere along the line the man at the gate has learned about Zeno and Parmenides, so that he understands the wider reference of his problem. I can't help thinking of the inventors of the two characters: Tate got a good education at Vanderbilt, Fitzgerald an indifferent one at Princeton.

The beginnings of the Agrarian movement—led by four of the Fugitives (Davidson, Ransom, Tate, and Warren) and eight other southerners—belong to the same period as the first draft of the "Ode to the Confederate Dead." A Tennessee law signed on March 18, 1925, prohibited the teaching of evolution in the tax-supported schools of the state. That summer old William Jennings Bryan's advocacy of the law in Dayton, Tennessee, made the state and the South the butt of easy ridicule throughout the country. Practically at the moment of the Fugitives' success at doing their bit for American letters in the South the Dayton trials were making it a laughingstock and worse—a place of ignoramuses and bigots. It was much as if, in 1963, a Birmingham, Alabama, poet were to be awakened by dynamite. What could he do but get out? At the time of the Dayton trials Tate had already, as he thought, escaped the South, and was rationalizing his course of action as the only one possible for a writer of southern birth. But in March 1926 he wrote Davidson that he had an idea for an essay on fundamentalism. In it he would "define the rights of both parties, science and religion," and he added that he was afraid "that science has very little to say for itself." He never wrote the essay though he did review *The Decline of the West* for the *Nation* under the title "Fundamentalism." In any case, Mrs. Cowan is surely right when she says that northern ridicule of the Dayton trials moved Tate in the direction of a defense of the South when before he was on the side of its critics.

On March 1, 1927, Tate wrote Davidson that he had "attacked the South for the last time, except in so far as it may be necessary to point out that the chief defect the Old South had was that in it which produced, through whatever cause, the New South." Some of the Fugitives were about to discover the serpent in the garden disguised as science and industrialism. Later in the same month Tate was proposing to Ransom an idea for a Southern Symposium—a collection of poems and stories which would show the world what the South really stood for. But Ransom, doubting that he and Tate could find many such poems and stories ("In the Old South the life aesthetic was actually realized, and there are the fewer object-lessons in its specific art"), proposed instead a collection of essays celebrating an agrarian as against an industrial society. Tate must have agreed to this; the result, three years later, was *I'll Take My Stand: The South and the Agrarian Tradition*, by Twelve Southerners—"an escapade," Ransom called it in 1959, "the last fling of our intellectual youth."

In 1925 Tate had set for himself a program of reading in southern history, and the fruits of this are his biographies of Stonewall Jackson (1928) and Jefferson Davis (1929). He also helped negotiate a contract between Robert Penn Warren and the publishers Payson and Clark for the writing of a biography of John Brown. An understanding of what was going on here is crucial to an understanding of Tate's later development.

As Tate saw the matter, the religion of the self-sufficiency of political man, the notion that man can fulfill his destiny solely through his political institutions, went into action during the American Civil War and won decisively. It has been winning all over the world ever since, though (I say this on my own) the greatly increased power of a barbarian version of it has tempered and gentled the American version. Among the Twelve Southerners, Andrew Lytle, Tate, and Warren had wanted to call the Agrarian manifesto "A Tract against Communism," but they were a minority; Yankeedom was enough of a Goliath for these Davids to take on without throwing the Bolsheviks into the bargain.

The religion of the self-sufficiency of political man was not a Yankee or even an American invention; but, according to Tate, the North really believed in it and the South did not. The South was defeated, Tate said, because it did not possess "a sufficient faith in its own kind of God." This is an almost hopelessly old-fashioned way to write history, and some students of Tate's work have been quick to apologize for it, pointing out, for example, that both his biographies are labeled "narratives." But I would question the need of apologies. Couldn't he believe his thesis all the more for its unprovability by statistical methods? Tate's way of writing history is the same as Gibbon's, the same as Milton's in the last two books of *Paradise Lost*, and the same as St. Augustine's in *The City of God*. Civilizations rise and fall as they hold fast to or lose an active faith.

In Tate's version it is a little as if the Civil War had been a conflict between Yeats's men of passionate intensity and men who lack all conviction. It is of course more complicated than that and more interesting. For one thing, the division was not strictly North and South; there was that midwesterner who is reported to have said to a southerner: "We should have fit them easterners with their little paper collars." There were also men of passionate intensity on both sides. Representative of these were John Brown and Stonewall Jackson: both martyrs, witnesses to their beliefs. In Tate's two biographies Jackson is shown to be as fanatical as Brown but he was a "good soldier," subordinate to Lee, and Lee in turn subordinated himself to President Jefferson Davis, who represents for Tate everything wrong with the South. His rise was without adversity, he complained constantly of "dyspepsia," he was obsessed to the end with his phantom Army Departments, even a "trans-Mississippi" one, and he treated Jackson and Lee as if they were secret weapons too terrible to use. He conducted the war as if he wanted to lose it, or if not lose it at least keep it going until the Old World came to his aid. As if Europe cared a straw about the society which Tate described fairly as "feudal, but without a feudal religion, and hence only semi-feudal." Europe, even Catholic Europe, had been busy for some time defeudalizing itself. Why should not the South do the same? The Agrarians could not stop this process, nor did they want to restore anything unrestorable. "I never thought of Agrarianism as a restoration of anything in the Old South," Tate has said. "I saw it as something to be created ... not only in the South ... but in the moral and religious outlook of Western man."

—George Hemphill. *Allen Tate* (Minneapolis: University of Minnesota, 1964): 12–17.

Ferman Bishop on Tate's Revision Process

[Ferman Bishop is the author of *Henry Adams* and, at the time he wrote *Allen Tate*, was on the faculty of Illinois State University. In the excerpt, Bishop compares earlier drafts of the poem to elucidate Tate's intent.]

I "Ode to the Confederate Dead"

In any survey of Tate's work, it is impossible to ignore the "Ode to the Confederate Dead." The analyses of Tate himself and of his critics have established it as the best known of his works. But they have also tended to render additional criticism difficult. After a brilliant critic like Tate has written on his own poem, what more is one to say? He himself perhaps provides the answer in his discussion of the relationship of the author and his reader: "... as a poet, my concern is the experience I hope the reader will have in reading the poem."[1] Each reading, in this view, must have its moment, however brief, of illumination. Tate's essay on his own poem need not be regarded as having done any more than what an extraordinarily gifted critic could do. There must always remain room for another point of view.

A technique of which Tate made relatively little use in

"Narcissus as Narcissus" is the comparative study of earlier and later versions of the poem. As a poet, he would naturally wish to stress the final form of his expression, and it would be only natural to avoid or even to suppress earlier versions of the poem. Certainly any judgment on the poem should be made on the author's final choice of expression. But when the earlier version help to illuminate the later one, it would seem to make a valuable adjunct for the reader.

Even small changes in a poem like "Ode to the Confederate Dead" are likely to be quite significant because all versions of the poem are focused through the mind of a perceiving consciousness. What the man in the poem says is always a part of a much larger and more complex entity—the whole mind of the man himself. And his mind in turn is a small indicator of a much larger and still more complex entity—the mind of man in the twentieth century. And this mind itself is only a part of the mind of mankind. For these reasons, the displacement of a phrase has much larger implications than might appear at first sight—so large, in fact, that probably no one could see far enough to encompass them all. It was no false modesty that led Tate to declare that he felt the poem beyond his powers; it is literally beyond the powers of any man. And this, of course, is its fascination.

As he himself points out, this poem is about solipsism:[2] the belief that the individual creates the world in perceiving it. The need for such an outlook is perhaps derived from the problem of the locked-in ego of modern man, a theme which Tate would have found "in the air," though one notably emphasized in the final section of *The Waste Land*. In the "Ode to the Confederate Dead," Tate dramatizes this problem by presenting the feelings of a modern man who is being forced to face his essential isolation. This Tate accomplishes by having him encounter a set of symbols, the chief of which is a Confederate cemetery. There follows a record of the stream-of-consciousness which ensues, proceeding from initial quietness through rising intensity to a climax, and finally ending in a denouement expressing his acceptance of his modern condition. The advantage of this arrangement is that it frees the utterance for a presentation of the full emotional-logical complexity of the man's situation. Being thus free, the utterance demands the facing of all the complexities inherent in each of the symbols. The content of the poem, therefore, is enormous—so great that no single reading could encompass it all.

The title in the earliest versions of the "Ode to the Confederate Dead" is amplified by the dates "1861–1865," which appear immediately beneath.[3] This device, though apparently insignificant, hints of a stronger tendency to memorialize the dead Confederates than in the later version of the poem. This would seem to give the man at the Confederate graves a stronger reason for his solipsistic contemplation than later seemed necessary. The speaker in the final version of the poem, being markedly more philosophical than his earlier counterpart, does not need to live by his impulses as much as a man who has not reflected on his experience.

In the second line of the earlier version, the headstones are said to "barter their names to the element," instead of the later "yield."[4] The use of a figure from trade implies that the speaker is a man of action. But unfortunately a long meditation does not seem particularly appropriate to such a man. Meditation for him might seem sentimental and insincere. Perhaps he would not be self-conscious enough to be concerned much with the problem of identity. For all of these reasons, Tate's changes make a considerable improvement.

The speaker's outlook on nature provides one of the most important means of indicating the quality of his mind. Like the Romantics, he relies on personification. Unlike them, he seasons his expression with figures expressive of mechanism: "The wind whirrs without recollection." The balance between these two sides of the speaker's mind came in for considerable attention in the process of revision. In the original version, nature's "sacrament" was opposed to the "sinkage" of death. The figure is much more mechanical than the final one of the "seasonal eternity of death." Much the same kind of change transformed the earlier "their business in the vast breath." That speaker could only interpret nature in the vocabulary of commerce. In the later poem a personification of heaven suggests the range of the speaker's comprehension. But his expression is ambiguous enough to allow for the doubts of modern man in his search for a controlling principle in the universe.

In the second section of the poem, the later version adds the two lines, "From the inexhaustible bodies that are not / Dead, but feed the grass row after rich row." The speaker's meditation concerns the inability of man's physical being to resist the effect of time. All the men in the cemetery are lying there without individual identities: they are merely "memories" of mass actions. Their present identities are merged in the concept "Confederate"; and this identification is interesting to the observer because he, too, is merged in some such grouping of men. The added lines may seem to avoid this problem and to express a romantic individualism like that of Whitman. But paradoxically, they say perhaps what they least expect to say: that the speaker fears that the bodies are capable of being exhausted. They are part indeed of the circular process of nature, but in its operation individual identity is eventually obliterated. With this change in the original context, the antagonism expressed in the second section between time personified in "November" and the idealization of mankind in the stone angels becomes more comprehensible. Time is conceived of as freedom of opportunity as opposed to the determinism of idealization. The speaker implies that the fixity of the idealization, the overstressing of the purely rational is at the heart of the spiritual illness of modern man.

Both versions of the poem agree in their stress on the ability of the idealization to drive the individual back upon his primitive impulses, symbolized by the crab. But the emphasis in the later version is stronger:

> The brute curiosity of an angel's stare
> Turns you, like them, to stone,
> Transforms the heaving air
> Till plunged to a heavier world below
> You shift your sea-space blindly
> Heaving, turning like the blind crab.

Whereas the earlier speaker was passive and unresisting, the later uses figures of motion. The heaving and turning are primitive and apparently futile, but they give the perceiver at least the benefit of some action. Yet his identification with the crab proclaims his awareness of the limitations upon the man of "locked-in ego."

The refrain which follows the second section is the first of four added at the suggestion of Hart Crane. It lends emphasis to the Whitmanesque interpretation of the leaves as individuals: "Dazed by the wind, only the wind / The leaves flying, plunge." Though the leaves seem at first glance to be wholly determined, they apparently have the choice between being destroyed and self-destruction. To the fascination of this possibility is added that of the esthetic qualities of the leaf on its final plunge. At this juncture the speaker, though aware of the problems of his world, still seems to have confidence in his outlook of individualism.

The next section, changed very little in revision, begins a comparison:

> You know who have waited by the wall
> The twilight certainty of an animal,
> Those midnight restitutions of the blood
> You know—the immitigable pines, the smoky frieze
> Of the sky, the sudden call: you know the rage,
> The cold pool left by the mounting flood,
> Of muted Zeno and Parmenides.

Apparently the speaker is addressing Tiresias, who waited by the wall of Thebes; and he feels that his own waiting here for illumination makes him in some respect identical with the ancient Greek. This modern man knows that the Greek's central problem is also his own: the problem of man. Tiresias is equipped to understand, and the speaker emphasizes the range of his experience.

He starts at the most primitive level—the animal. But the "restitutions of the blood" are precisely what modern man is incapable of achieving. As a further element in his catalogue, the pines are "immitigable" because he is projecting into them his own emotional need for permanence in nature. The "smoky frieze of the sky" likewise interprets nature in terms of the speaker's emotional need—this time to make it comprehensible within the framework of his inheritance of ideas from the Graeco-Roman world. The "cold pool left by the mounting flood" suggests a still higher need based on the problems of permanence and change. This idea is especially reinforced by the mention of Heraclitus (instead of Zeno) in the original version. Seemingly, the original speaker had in mind the conflict between the stress on becoming in Heraclitus and on being in Parmenides. The lack of agreement between those ancient philosophers finds its counterpart in the mind of twentieth-century man. Tate's change in the final version of the poem from Heraclitus to Zeno and the addition of the line "The cold pool left by the mounting flood" emphasizes the likeness of these ancient philosophers in skepticism. And in this quality they are especially modern.

Tiresias, knowing all, understands the close balance of life and death. In the earlier version of the poem he is said to praise the "immodest circumstance" of those who fall. But certainly "arrogant" in the later version conveys much more clearly the suggestion of the death wish in the speaker. His sense of futility was markedly emphasized in the shift from the line of the Fugitive anthology, "Here at this stile, once more, you know It all," to "Here by the sagging gate, stopped by the wall."

The section beginning "Turn your eyes to the immoderate past" represents momentary elation on the part of the speaker as he glimpses the possibilities of free choice given to the dead Confederates. The changes incorporated into the later versions of the section seem mostly intended to emphasize this element of free choice. The line "Find there the inscrutable infantry rising." The possibility of freedom of will seems much greater in the second, especially because of the repetition of "turn" from the preceding line. And earlier versions of the poem compared the infantry with "The demons out of the earth," an apparent reference to the demons of Gadarene, which Matthew, Mark, and Luke agree in calling inhabitants of the tombs. In the final version of the poem, the line became "Demons out of the earth." This change removes the deterministic implications of the Biblical story and shifts the speaker's emphasis to the freedom of choice of the avenging spirits.

When the speaker begins to call the famous Civil War names, he is attempting to find meaning in the concreteness of the individuals and events of that struggle. Because he resists the deterministic implications of mass movements or gatherings of men, he tries to find it in the qualities of men like Jackson and in deeds such as those of Albert Sidney Johnston at Shiloh. The earlier speaker concluded his meditation with, "In the orient of that economy / You have cursed the setting sun." Both "orient" and "economy" are used figuratively—the one for "east" and the other for "arrangement" or "dispensation." And the idea seems appropriate for Tiresias, whose foreknowledge must have caused him to regret the passing of such a race of emotionally integrated men. But the later version: "Lost in that orient of the thick-and-fast / You will curse the setting sun" allows the speaker to project his own ideas into the mind of Tiresias. Psychologically, it is much the more appropriate utterance. And poetically, the omission of "economy" is a great gain, for its connotations of the world of affairs remain with it even in another context.

The same kind of alteration is to be seen in the handling of the concept of silence in the "mummy" section. In the earlier version it was said to "engulf"; in the latter, to "smother." Because the speaker is given to personification as a means of understanding, the later version seems more appropriate. The mummy, which appears in both versions, suggests very well the personal element in the mind of the speaker. It also raises many problems: the decline of civilizations, the futility of man's effort to defeat the operation of time, the relationship of man and the hereafter. But the speaker in the earlier version is far more conscious of his figure: he makes it a simile and adds "whose niche / Lacks aperture." In later versions this idea is pruned away, and the figure stands alone, far more effective than when embellished. The deletion also allows for the close juxtaposition of mummy and hound bitch, also a later addition. Both express the tension between freedom and necessity which is uppermost in the speaker's mind. And both are reinforced by the religious tones of the "salt of their blood" section, which implies one solution in the speaker's mind for the problem of necessity.

Unsatisfied, the speaker turns his questions toward the individual. The speaker of the earlier version says: "What shall we say of the dirty sons / Whose legs and arms, guts, heads and teeth / Stretched out the justice of efficiency?" And in the final version, these lines are replaced by:

> What shall we say of the bones, unclean,
> Whose verdurous anonymity will grow?
> The ragged arms, the ragged heads and eyes
> Lost in these acres of the insane green?

Both are questions about the problem of identity. The true essence of the men has been merged with something larger, as suggested by the mingling of the "salt of their blood" with the ocean. But there remains the question of the individual. His meaning must have to do not only with the "malignant purity" of his ideal essence, but with his uncleanness as well. The first speaker solves his problem by using a catalogue of anatomical detail. The effect intended is that of shock. But in the final version, Tate mitigates the starkness of this effect by allowing his speaker to merge the soldiers with the nature in which they rest. Nature and the memory of the men are transformed together. The personification is suitable to his solipsism, and his reverie does seem more philosophically satisfying than that of the first speaker. But this gain is bought at the risk of seeming slightly sentimental. For the speaker is obviously thinking of himself and his plight at also being lost in the "acres of the insane green."

The passage which follows, common to all versions of the poem, brings in spiders, owl, and willows. These conventional death symbols all have overtones of determinism. They imply the history of which the soldiers are a part; it is as important a part of their meaning as their future. Still another aspect of their meaning is suggested in the synesthesia of "invisible lyric."

The physical and the spiritual are mysteriously brought into relationship even in the song of the screech owl.

The next sections concern the consequences of the meditation in the graveyard. In the earlier version, the transition is made rather abruptly:

> We have not sung, we shall not ever sing
> In the improbable mist of nightfall
> Which flies on multiple wing;
> It has only a beginning and an end;
> And in between the ends of distraction
> Lurks mute speculation, the patient curse
> That stones the eyes, or like the jaguar leaps
> For the jaguar's image in a jungle pool, his victim.

This modern man realizes that he cannot achieve that creativity which will give meaning to the physical and spiritual sides of his nature. His is the problem of an overemphasis on a sterile rationality, which eventuates in skepticism. Because his philosophical outlook requires a projection of himself into what he perceives, his use of the insect figure is significant. It implies a parody of human consciousness and human creativity. Perhaps he can sing, but only with a voice which emphasizes, even more than the voice of the screech-owl, his sterility. The figure of the jaguar follows appropriately in his meditation because he is obviously post-Darwinian in thought. It implies the individualism that must result from his skepticism—an individualism that is ultimately self-destructive.

The final version of this section employs the same figures, somewhat rearranged:

> We shall say only the leaves whispering
> In the improbable mist of nightfall
> That flies on multiple wing;
> Night is the beginning and the end
> And in between the ends of distraction
> Waits mute speculation, the patient curse
> That stones the eyes, or like the jaguar leaps
> For his own image in a jungle pool, his victim.

For this speaker, the possibility of creativeness seems much more remote than for his predecessor. He can only contemplate. The voice of the leaves is reduced to a mere whisper; he implies that there is for him no individual choice, only the determinism of science. Because he can have only a limited possibility of significant action, his capacity for struggle is likewise limited. If this is true, then he must be a lesser man than his predecessor. He may even be a sentimentalist who uses his philosophy as an excuse to avoid the possibility of action.

But in the section of the poem which follows, he is partially saved, as was his predecessor, by "knowledge carried to the heart"—his direct apprehension of the world of symbols. Despite the poet's word to the contrary, the speaker seems anything but resigned to the idea that the grave is all. The answers to his questions about the grave seem clearly to be negative, especially in light of the adjective in "the ravenous grave."

The last section in the first version of the poem began: "Leave now / The turnstile and the decomposing wall." In the final version of the poem, this became: "Leave now / The shut gate and the decomposing wall." The finality of the observer's statement seems much stronger in the later version. The turnstile as a form of the wheel is an effective symbol of determinism. But it also implies mechanism, one feature of which is the idea of reversibility. The "shut gate" carries the idea of finality much more strongly. The Confederate cemetery thereby becomes a kind of Eden from which man is finally locked out. And the figure of the serpent, to which the speakers mind now turns, seems natural in this context. It is linked not only with time, but also with knowledge and with evil. The fact that it is a "gentle serpent"—a silkworm—allows it to suggest the thread of life and the Fates as well as scientific determinism.

The last line of the early version of the poem was: "See him—what he knows—he knows it all!" In the final version, it becomes: "Sentinel of the grave who counts us all!" The first version makes explicit the symbolism of the serpent-silkworm; the later assumes it. Perhaps the most subtle feature of the final version is its use of the pronoun, which personifies the grave. By identifying himself with the grave, the speaker has comprehended it. His is a personification appropriate to a counting man of modern science. Yet the tone is matter of fact, and the speaker seems resigned.

Tate's achievement—and it goes without saying that he must be judged on the final version of his poem—is both philosophical and esthetic. The careful selection of the concrete materials of his poem enables him to suggest the vast complexity of problems which beset modern man. And his speaker's mind is such as to encompass a set of reactions to these problems and to suggest an adjustment to his age possible for twentieth-century man. In a sense this might be described as bravery. Caught up in the history, philosophy, and science of his age, he might easily have become self-pitying. But his figures show a high degree of control. Perhaps it is not too much to find him brave in a sense that few of Hemingway's characters ever are. For Tate required not only that the intellect be placed under control, but the emotions as well.

Notes

1. *Selected Poems* (New York, 1937), p. ix.
2. "Narcissus as Narcissus," *Collected Essays*, p. 250.
3. *Mr. Pope and Other Poems*, p. 33.
4. *Poems*, p. 19.

—Ferman Bishop. *Allen Tate* (New York: Twayne Publishers, Inc., 1967): 84–93.

Radcliffe Squires Explicates the Poem

[J. Radcliffe Squires (1918–1993) was Professor Emeritus of English at the University of Michigan. He wrote a number of significant biographical and critical works focusing of 20th-century writers. He is the author of *Allen Tate: A Literary Biography*, and the editor of an important collection of essays, *Allen Tate and His Work*, and the editor of *Michigan Quarterly Review* throughout much of the 1970s. He wrote seven books of poetry and numerous critical works, including *The Loyalties of Robinson Jeffers* and *The Major Themes of Robert Frost*. Here, Squires' explication, taken from the first biography of the poet, ties together biographical aspects with intention and technique.]

By reason of its intrinsic importance the "Ode to the Confederate Dead" merits an approach as complicated as the poem and its backgrounds are complicated. To talk about it at all is like stripping an artichoke toward its heart. One begins at the outside because that is where one has to begin, and every bract is tipped with a thorn. The poem is the record of a failure, yet what caution must be observed with the word "failure." For it means an incompetence to create of experience, past and present, the kind of great and relevant expression which one associates with blossoming cultures, with the drama of Sophocles, for example. For Tate the age had no particular sense of purpose; its religion had deteriorated to social philosophy; hence he doubted that an artist could produce a statement incorporating a whole, steady vision. Thus he was stuck with only the possibly eccentric, probably small and scattered impressions of a subjective vision. Such was the extension of his belief that poetry should be concerned with "the aspect of things." But one must go back even further to his earlier intuitions about poetry. Tate had, it would seem, as early as 1922, begun to worry about whether art could fully succeed in embodying the age. But he hoped it could. In a not very good poem entitled "On a Portrait of Hart Crane," published in *The Double-Dealer* he asserts that though he has not yet "clasped" the hand of Crane he hopes to learn from him the way of "vision." "Vision" has an obvious relationship to "the aspect of things." What Tate ironically learned from Hart Crane was that a merely personal vision would not work well enough: that Crane himself could not weld together by vision a split view of America, could not hold together Whitman's democratic vistas and Poe's inverted image of the House of Usher. And so "vision," which is, after all, an aggrandizement of personality, failed. This failure partly accounts for Tate's concern with the past, for the past came to represent tradition. Tradition itself of course is seen to be significant because of continuities of idea, religion, and purpose in culture—all the things that Dante or Vergil could press into their art. But Tate could not fully believe in his own Southern tradition, for, as we have seen, it was, while preferable in his view to a New England tradition, fragmented and imperfect. Left with little confidence, he began to insist that great art could not be produced in the twentieth century. By 1927, Yvor Winters, with whom Tate had begun a correspondence, felt that he must chide Tate for feeling that the artist needed a total explanation of the whole universe. He further observed that this demand could only lead to paralysis, and that at any rate the view was absurd in one whose capacity to write significant poetry was of the highest order.[13]

Against this background of uncertainty and exasperation—not against a background of Southern Agrarianism—Tate wrote his ode. In it he does not celebrate the Confederate dead; he records his inability to celebrate. In short, he yields quite purely to a subjective treatment, or, to use the word Tate himself would have employed at the time, he yields to a poetry of mere "sensibility."

Tate has told us a number of valuable things about the poem in his essay "Narcissus as Narcissus" (1938). The essay originated in response to a request from Norman Holmes Pearson for commentary on the poem which he wanted to include in *The Oxford Anthology of American Literature* (1938). It grew beyond reasonable bounds for that purpose, though two paragraphs from the essay were published by Pearson as a note to the poem. Those paragraphs still serve their purpose:

> The structure of the Ode is simple. Figure to yourself a man stopping at the gate of a Confederate graveyard on a late autumn afternoon. The leaves are falling; his first impressions bring him the "rumor of mortality"; and the desolation barely allows him, at the beginning of the second stanza, the conventionally heroic surmise that the dead will enrich the earth, "where these memories grow." From those quoted words to the end of that passage he pauses for a baroque meditation on the ravages of time, concluding with the figure of the "blind crab." This creature has mobility but no direction, energy, but from the human point of view, no purposeful world to use it in: in the entire poem there are only two explicit symbols for the locked-in ego; the crab is the first and less explicit symbol, a mere hint, a planting of the idea that will become overt in its second instance—the jaguar towards the end. The crab is the first intimation of the nature of the moral conflict upon which the drama of the poem develops: the cut-offness of the modern "intellectual man" from the world.

> The next long passage or "strophe" beginning "You know who have waited by the wall," states the other term of the conflict. It is the theme of heroism, not merely moral heroism, but heroism in the grand style, elevating even death from mere physical dissolution into a formal ritual: this heroism is a formal ebullience of the human spirit in an entire society, not private, romantic illusion—something better than moral heroism, great as that may be, for moral heroism, being personal and individual, may be achieved by certain men in all ages, even ages of decadence. But the late Hart Crane's commentary, in a letter, is better than any I can make; he described the theme as the "theme of chivalry, a tradition of excess (not literally excess, rather active faith) which cannot be perpetuated in the fragmentary cosmos of today—'those desires which should be yours tomorrow,' but which, you know; will not persist nor find any way into action."

The essay also discloses the poetic procedures of the poem, the mounting rhythm, the varied lengths of the iambic lines, the shock tactics of unexpected rhymes. These disclosures are fascinating. It may be doubted that most readers could on their own uncover the ploys and gambits Tate extended. That is of slight importance. As W.H. Auden has said, the poet himself is the supreme expert on his own devices; no one can come up to him. One is aware, however dumbly, of form, music, device and of the organization of all of these things. One might be ignorant of the turnings Tate lathed into the lines of the "Ode," but he could not miss the severe music that falls and rises like the medieval *sequentia*. He might go innocent of the rhyme set like a trap, but he does not go innocent of the shock of both sound and image. Since Tate tells us as much as he does and speaks from such incontrovertible authority, there is little to add. Here is that little.

"Ode to the Confederate Dead" has been revised several times. The version quoted here is the final one (1936)—a bad choice with respect to chronology, yet a choice made inevitable by the fact that the poem is what it became. Anyway, except for the addition of a varied refrain, the emendations are not very extensive. The refrain was added in 1930, as Tate tells us, to pace the poem and render "quite plain the subjective character of the poem throughout." It first appears as follows:

Dazed by the wind, only the wind
The leaves flying, plunge.

There are variations but all of them keep the wind-driven leaves.

This leaf-refrain, though added almost five years after the first draft of the poem, does not intrude some image which occurred to Tate in greater maturity. On the contrary, the image may be found in one form or another, even in this specific form, in poems earlier than "Ode to the Confederate Dead." In the fourth issue of *The Fugitive*, a sonnet entitled "These Deathy Leaves" imagistically counterpoises the falling leaves against love and rebirth. The autumnal theme and image are, of course, too commonplace to constitute overpowering evidence of anything at all. Yet the image does seem obsessive with Tate. In the very next issue of *The Fugitive* (February–March 1923) the image occurs again in the poem "Teeth," and here the context is not that of rebirth but despondency and social decay:

No music comes to sorrow like a thief,
  No twitter of birds, as in Spring, for eucharist;
Only the soft thrust of a falling leaf
  And in the mind the bloodless lips of Christ.

The "bloodless lips of Christ" haunt Tate's poetry for two decades. The "soft thrust of a falling leaf" is ancestor to the leaves that fall, plunging in the Ode. And the image means more in Tate's poetry than it superficially seems to mean.

Throughout his verse, images of nature appear. These are seldom simple or innocent—the peeled aster in "Death of Little Boys" is exemplary of the kind. These images jut from the poems with a curious sort of impertinence. Not that they do not bring feeling to the poems, not that they cannot be justified by various relationships, but that they are cold and ecdemic. They are cold and ecdemic because they propose a nature that is going its way alone, separate from man and from the passions or sentiments of the poet. The natural observation can be emblematic of emotion or idea in Tate's poetry, but only by an *accident* of analogy. One may contrast this impression with that which he derives from Frost's analogies between self and nature, analogies which have about them an air of providence and inevitability. That may be a way of saying that Tate, unlike Frost, has never admired Emersonian transcendentalism. Whatever the reason, nature in Tate's poetry takes on an aspect of idiocy over which he attempts to triumph with a universalizing adjective, a fixative, one might say, as in the phrase "ambitious November" from the "Ode." The attribution "ambitious," reminiscent of T.S. Eliot's *depraved* May or *cruelest* April, is not pathetic fallacy so much as ratiocinative fallacy, for it does not seek to draw nature into a relationship of feeling; it seeks to set it apart in an ideal attitude. One further observation on this score. The isolation from the natural environment is one which further isolates the speaker in the "Ode" and therefore more certainly condemns him to his awareness only of the aspect of things. To what degree the subjective isolation extends may be seen in the third variation of the refrain, introduced by the line "You will curse the setting sun":

> Cursing only the leaves crying
> Like an old man in a storm.

It is difficult here to avoid remembering King Lear and the subjective monomania in which he is imprisoned.

The speaker of the poem is imprisoned in the self and imprisoned therefore in darkness; the "Ode" is the darkest of Tate's poems, containing not a single image of light. That is noteworthy in a poem by a poet who is addicted to images of light. No, what one finds is "blind crab," "twilight certainty," "midnight restitutions," "willows without light." "Night is the beginning and the end," we are told. It is not surprising. As indicated earlier, the poem was written in a spirit of disillusionment in Hart Crane's faith in vision. But the disillusionment probably goes back at least a year earlier. The poem "Ignis Fatuus" (1925) shows a rejection of romantic vision. One says "romantic" because the fool's fire in the poem is associated with "fierce latinity." In the first stanza Tate writes:

> In the twilight of my audacity
> I saw you flee the world, the burnt highways

Of summer gave up their light: I
Followed you with the uncommon span
Of fear supported and disbursed eyes

In the last stanza he writes:

To the green tissue of the subterranean
Worm I have come back, two-handed from
The chase, and empty. I have pondered it
Carefully, and asked: Where is the light
When the pigeon moults his ease
Or exile utters the creed of memory?
So much for vision at this point in Tate's career.

There is no light, then, in the "Ode to the Confederate Dead." Only the dark of self, which knows "the rage, / The cold pool left by the mounting flood, / Of muted Zeno and Parmenides," those Eleatic solipsists for whom reality was nothing more than illusion created within the mind. Two years before, Tate had feared that this might be the beginning and end of all poetry, for he had written in an editorial in *The Fugitive* for April 1924 that "the Modern poet might tell you that his only possible themes are the manifold projections and tangents of his own perception. It is the age of the Sophist."

If the "Ode," with its yielding to the theme of the self in an age without faith, is the blackest of Tate's poems, it nevertheless, by going down so deeply to the bedrock of his despair, prepared the way for future reconsiderations of the theme, efforts to dispel the shades of Zeno and Parmenides. Some of these efforts were to prove successful, and the more successful were to prove to be Tate's loftiest poems. Yet the impression must not stand that "Ode to the Confederate Dead" wants stature. One must argue its case at the highest level. Indeed, it belongs with some of the finest poems of the century, and it belongs with them because it shows with them its intense, though separate, treatment of the same thematic material. These poems must include T.S. Eliot's "The Love Song of J. Alfred Prufrock," Paul Valéry's "Marine Cemetery," and Wallace Stevens' "Sunday Morning." Each of these poems, though Eliot's is a dramatic monologue and

Stevens' is a multi-voiced argument, is a meditation upon the relationship between subjective and objective worlds. For Eliot's agonist the inner world cannot pierce into an outer world. Valéry, like Tate, mentions "cruel Zeno" who freezes the world in subjective vision, but then goes on to suppose the subjective vision can give movement to existence. Stevens also ends confident of a subjective vision which he believes offers a metaphysics parallel to the clutter of objective phenomena, so that death is not only the natural but also the mystical mother of beauty. Tate's "Ode to the Confederate Dead" is bleaker than Eliot's poem, less humanly arrogant than Valéry's or Stevens', less willing to soften or dilute its theme. Though it was written later than the others, it should be read before them. For the theme behind his poem is the theme of the others, and it is an old theme: the *vanitas* about which St. Augustine knew everything.

Perhaps "Ode to the Confederate Dead" got too much attached to Tate's name—with the result that his finer poems have been disregarded. But it brought him early fame. This was a fame that Tate, the recipient of a Guggenheim award in 1928, took with him to Europe. He also took with him the unresolved dilemma of "Ode to the Confederate Dead," his question, "What shall we say who have carried knowledge to the heart?" He meant, how shall the poetic self speak nobly and publicly of the past or present or of things to come? He had without knowing it answered his own question. At the end of the "Ode," he hears the silkworm eating mulberry leaves, and calls that creature a "gentle serpent" who is "Sentinel of the grave who counts us all." In "Narcissus as Narcissus" this serpent is explained as the universal symbol of "time." Of course it is, but if Tate had thought longer about his symbol he might have remembered that when Aeneas prays at his father's grave, a serpent wriggles up from the earth. That serpent was the spirit of his lineage, the spirit of the past, present, and future of the house.

NOTE

13. M.D. Bradford, *Rumors of Mortality* (Dallas, 1969), p. 27.

—Radcliffe Squires. *Allen Tate: A Literary Biography* (New York: Bobbs Merrill Company, Inc., 1971): 75–82.

Robert S. Dupree on Tate's Parody of Religious Ideals

[Robert S. Dupree is Professor of English at the University of Dallas, where he is also Director of Libraries/Research. He is the author of *Allen Tate and the Augustinian Imagination*, as well as co-editor, with Terence Dawson, of *Seventeenth-Century English Poetry: The Annotated Anthology*. In this excerpt, Dupree points out the abundant contradictions and parodies that result in the speaker's crisis, unresolved by his indecision.]

These two polarities—death and the self—are the tensional basis for the kind of conflict between deterministic pessimism and radical solipsism Tate depicts in "Ode to the Confederate Dead." The first stanza shows a natural order that is dominated by the closed system of "the seasonal eternity of death." The whole passage is a picture of a world with a kind of Spenglerian destiny that ignores the presence of man. There are suggestions of a system of rewards and punishments, such as might make up some mythical order of justice, but nature offers only the salvation that comes with total effacement. What is lacking is any sense of individual continuity that might break out of the terrible cycle. The stone memorials placed over the graves "yield their names" with "strict impunity." Their loss of memory will go unpunished and uncorrected. The wind shows no signs of "recollection"—the poet puns on the scattering effect of wind on the leaves in the "riven troughs" as well as the mindless energy of its whirr. The leaves themselves are "splayed," never again to be made whole; they are part of nature's "casual sacrament," an accidental rather than an intentional communion. (The word "casual" suggests the "fall" of the leaves by association with Latin casus.) The falling leaves have long been images of human mortality, from Homer, Virgil, and Dante to Shelley; but these leaves also take on the imagined quality of damned beings. Part of the whole of things, they lose all individuality as they are "driven ... to their election in the vast breath." Like "The Subway," "Ode to the Confederate Dead" is a grim parody of traditional religious ideas of salvation tinged with overtones of predestinarian determinism.

If death dominates the first stanza, the self is prominent in the second. The protagonist of the poem attempts to break out of the terror of this organic cycle by thinking "of the autumns that have come and gone," but memory itself takes on the quality of the grass that feeds analogically on the dead bodies. The alternative to the closed temporal system that he views resides in some sort of spatial suspension, represented in part by the sculptured angels on the tombs. There is surely a suggestion in this passage of what Tate was later to call "the angelic imagination," an ability to penetrate into the essence of things without recourse to their sensual manifestations. The "brute curiosity of an angel's stare," which like the Gorgon's turns those who look on it to stone, is trapped in decaying matter, the "uncomfortable" statue assaulted by "the humors of the year." The split between body and mind is embodied in the art of the grave sculptor's angels as much as in the sensibility of the protagonist. Like the falling leaves, he too is "plunged to a heavier world below," a kind of mental hell in which, like Dante's damned shades, he exerts directionless and purposeless energies. (Tate's description of Phelps Putnam's heroes also comes to mind.)

The grim wit of Tate's language—the multiple shadings of words like "impunity," "recollection," "sacrament," "scrutiny," "rumor," "inexhaustible," "zeal," or "brute"—gives these first two stanzas an astonishing compactness and power. Their dense network of analogies denies poetically the assertion in the following refrain that the protagonist is seeing nothing more than fall leaves. What he knows that nature does not know is history and the pattern of things that comes through the memory as man's refusal to submit to mere despair. For unlike the fallen leaves, man continues to believe that he has a future.

You who have waited for the angry resolution
Of those desires that should be yours tomorrow,
You know the unimportant shrift of death
And praise the vision
And praise the arrogant circumstance
Of those who fall
Rank upon rank, hurried beyond decision—
Here by the sagging gate, stopped by the wall.

"Ambitious November" is answered by the arrogance of man himself; he will rush to his death without waiting for his place in the natural cycle of decay. It is this "immoderate past" that makes man "inscrutable," in answer to the mindless but "fierce scrutiny" of the sky. Though man cannot possess the stony detachment of the angelic self depicted on the statues, he does have a strange demonic energy that pulls him out of the earth. He knows the empty paradoxes of the mind—the puzzles of "muted Zeno and Parmenides" as they contemplate the nature of time and being. But he also knows the "twilight certainty of an animal." If Zeno's paradox would never allow the arrow to hit the target, death's efficacy in drawing all things to their destruction is indubitable. The struggle between self and death has reached an equilibrium in the protagonist's thoughts.

The late autumnal season of the poem and the setting sun that dominates its main scenes are traditional symbols of history and death. (Besides his correlation of the seasons and stages of historical growth and decay, Spengler's title—literally "Sunset of the West"—offers an obvious parallel.) What history provides is a memory of "that orient of the thick-and-fast" where action begins; but since the protagonist has been reduced to paralysis, "stopped by the wall" (death) and the "angel's stare" (self), he can only hover over the decaying transition point of the "sagging gate," the threshold of initiation into another life or state. Sight and sound, like time and space, are confused in him:

> You hear the shout, the crazy hemlocks point
> With troubled fingers to the silence which
> Smothers you, a mummy, in time.

The mummy is a particularly interesting image, since it can stand both for the ineffectiveness of a man wrapped in his embalming shroud and for the limited immortality of the body. Like the "old man in a storm," it is surrounded by the ravages of time yet remains a captive of space. Outside of time, like the mummy, the self has no freedom. This section of the poem is brought to a close by the image of the "hound bitch," a reminder of the ancient action of the hunt. She should be a symbol of vitality; now, however, she too is the quarry of death, lying "in a musty cellar." The end of the hunt is another manifestation of that loss of heroic energy which once drove the soldiers to their graves. The soldiers and the hound bitch live for the event and decay once the event is concluded. Still, their fate is better than the mummylike existence in time that has rendered the protagonist immobile.

What remains for modern man is that blank oneness of the universe which dissolves all into a "malignant purity" and a salty "oblivion" (examples of Tate's startling use of oxymoron). There is a radical shift, however, in the sixth stanza, and Tate himself has spoken of it as the beginning of the second main division of the poem, in "Narcissus as Narcissus." The progression is evidenced by the metrical movement, as he points out, but also by a shift in the pronoun from "you" to "we." Tate's final question to Spengler, "How shall we set about restoring the values that have been lost?" is already posed in this poem. The poet asks it of the young man who stands by the gate. For it is at this point that one becomes aware of some sort of community standing behind the protagonist, those "who count our days and bow / Our heads with a commemorial woe" during the public ceremonies offered for the dead. The ritualistic gestures are still carried on, though perhaps as a "grim felicity" that is a distinct decline from heroic action. What has changed in the perception the poem offers, however, is the image of nature: Before, nature was the inhuman cycle of a world without past or future. Now there is the suggestion of something in nature that recalls man's heroic energies:

> In a tangle of willows without light
> The singular screech-owl's tight
> Invisible lyric seeds the mind
> With the furious murmur of their chivalry.

This is an image different from the "brute curiosity" of the angel's stare and the mere sound of the wind. In the darkness where space has vanished, there is an aural suggestion of an energy with more direction than that of the "blind crab." It is crucial to see what has occurred in this and the following stanza.

The question that has been asked—"what shall we say of the

bones?"—is answered in the refrain—"We shall say only the leaves / Flying, plunge and expire." Those who merely go through the motions of the ritual of "grim felicity" can see nothing more than that "Night is the beginning and the end." They cannot speak because there is nothing to speak about. Birth and death are but "the ends of distraction," and between them is the "mute speculation" of Zeno and Parmenides and the angel's gorgonic stare, that "patient curse / That stones the eyes." The toothless dog is replaced by the energetic jaguar who "leaps / For his own image in a jungle pool, his victim." The cycle of nature has been replaced by the solipsistic self. The "mute speculation" is part of the "jungle pool" (a play on the Latin word for mirror, speculum, is hidden in the phrase). Vision and space, the counting of days, abstract stare, the setting sun, all these Spengler-like images are part of the symbolic paralysis that must be rejected for an acceptance of the aural and temporal dimensions of the memory, the understanding, and the will. The critical question is transformed at the end of the poem in a phrase that has become famous:

> What shall we say who have knowledge
> Carried to the heart? Shall we take the act
> To the grave? Shall we, more hopeful, set up the grave
> In the house? The ravenous grave?

This solution is the one Spengler seems to embrace, for his impressive array of organically growing and dying cultures adds up to nothing more than worship of the grave. By giving no final meaning to human history, Spengler falsifies his own premises. If human memory serves only as a means of collecting man's actions around the central fact of death, then human history has no significance at all. In Spengler the West has indeed begun to set up the grave in its own house.

The protagonist in "Ode to the Confederate Dead" stands between two communities, the city of the living and the city of the dead; but he does not know how to bring them together in any meaningful fashion. He has the kind of intuitive knowledge that has been "carried to the heart," but he is also haunted by the specter of abstract rationalism—"muted Zeno and Parmenides," who, like the jaguar, stare into the "cold pool" of a method that removes them from life and action. He never enters the cemetery; the gate remains shut to him at the end. He cannot participate in the kind of space occupied by the dead, and he is himself smothered in time. He is typical of the modern man in his mummylike condition. The only kind of immortality the modern mind can grasp is one that is a stopping of the natural cycle, an immobilization of all life processes.

The poem ends, as Tate emphasizes in his essay, with an image that complements the owl, that of the serpent. Like the ouroboros—that ancient figure of the snake biting its tail—it is a symbol of the relation of time to eternity. Equally significant is the command to the protagonist to leave the "shut gate and the decomposing wall." For he is not the poet, this man at the gate, but the skeptical historian who meditates on the past of Western civilization as though he were looking at a graveyard. The gate and the wall separate the living from the dead, but the two important "sounds" in the poem—the screech-owl's call and the rioting "tongue" of the "gentle serpent"—are appeals to some kind of life. That life is not the simple organic cycle of nature but something beyond it. As the figure of the serpent makes plain, it is the life of myth, of speech through the imagination that is neither mutely paralyzed like the mummy nor rendered as a meaningless noise in the buffeting of the leaves. By yielding to time and participating in the past through memory, man can at least survive through the makeshift devices of his secular imagination, even in a declining civilization. Nevertheless, "Ode to the Confederate Dead" does not offer, as Tate explains in his essay, a "practical solution ... for the edification of moralists," but it does imply that such a solution is possible. As Tate goes on to say, "To those who may identify the man at the gate with the author of the poem I would say: He differs from the author in not accepting a 'practical solution,' for the author's personal dilemma is perhaps not quite so exclusive as that of the meditating man."[23] It is the exclusive character of the dilemma that makes it difficult to resolve, for the alternative of science or religion at least offers the promise of a practical solution to the problem of acting in an alien universe. Unless the man at the gate can learn to see the choice between a nature dominated by mortality and a self locked in solipsism as a false presentation of alternatives, he cannot act in any decisive way.

NOTES

22. Allen Tate, Review of Phelps Putnam's *Trinc*, in *New Republic*, LIII, 76.
23. Allen Tate, "Narcissus as Narcissus," in *Essays*, 600.

—Robert S. Dupree. *Allen Tate and the Augustinian Imagination: A Study of Poetry* (Baton Rouge: Louisiana State University Press, 1983.): 46–51.

WILLIAM DORESKI ON THE CONTEXT OF TATE'S VOICE

[William Doreski's poetry has most recently appeared in *Notre Dame Review*, *Harvard Review*, *Atlanta Review*, *Barrow Street*, and *Birmingham Poetry Review*. He has published a critical study, *Robert Lowell's Shifting Colors*, as well as *The Modern Voice in American Poetry* and *The Years of Our Friendship: Robert Lowell and Allen Tate*, and two collections of poetry, *Suburban Light* and *Pianos in the Woods*. He teaches literature and creative writing at Keene State College in New Hampshire. In the following excerpt, Doreski looks for Lowell's tonal influences in Tate and describes the formal power of Tate's language.]

In a poetic era dominated by the first-person lyric voice, we might too quickly dismiss the utility of less immediate voices. Even by the 1950s, before the full onslaught of frankly autobiographical verse, some critics found Tate too repressed and too monotonous. One critic, writing in 1960, described Tate's poetry as "Notably intellectual, compressed to the point of ellipsis and even of obscurity, referential, bold in imagery, and often desperate in tone."[12] This accurately describes some of Tate's poems, but it overlooks his tonal range. Without looking ahead to Tate's openly autobiographical poetry of the 1950s, we see that the 1920s and 1930s poems have a range of feeling and tone akin to Eliot's, but without his incomparable virtuosity. The ironic bitterness of "Mr. Pope," the different, though perhaps equally ironic, grief of "Ode to the Confederate Dead," the satiric religiosity of "The Subway," and the philosophical and religious meditation of "Causerie" (a poem of enormous importance to Lowell's work of the 1940s) represent a tonal range greater than that generally credited to Tate. Some of his poems "leave us longing for the warm pulse of human blood and the feel of flesh,"[13] but the same has been said of Eliot's *Four Quartets*. Poetry is not always intended to be sensuous, much less sensual, yet the texture of the great "Ode to the Confederate Dead," like that of *Lycidas* and "Ode to the West Wind," its forebears, is sensuous in the way that only language at its most powerful can be:

> What shall we say of the bones, unclean,
> Whose verdurous anonymity will grow?
> The ragged arms, the ragged heads and eyes
> Lost in these acres of the insane green?
> The gray lean spiders come, they come and go;
> In a tangle of willows without light
> The singular screech-owl's tight
> Invisible lyric seeds the mind
> With the furious murmur of their chivalry.

The varied end rhyme scheme, repetitions, and internal rhymes lend momentum and inevitability, and the oxymorons ("verdurous anonymity," "furious murmur") give these lines the force of the irrational and undeniable rightness of language. Tate, at his best, displays a technical ability that is not merely virtuosity but the genuine poet's instinct for language that is true because of its sound not its content. The voice of this poem is uniquely Tate's, and in that most important sense, it is personal. As Lowell said of Tate, "His poems, even the slightest of them, are terribly personal. Out of splutter and shambling comes a killing eloquence."[14] Tate's poems are personal not because they are about himself but because no one else could have written them; in reaction against what he came to call "mass language," he has, to some degree, freed his language from merely conventional reference.[15] For this same kind of individuality,

Tate admired Hart Crane. If Crane was the more eloquent poet, it was because he was even more fearless in freeing his language from easy literalness. In this way, Bradbury's worry about Tate's "ellipsis" and "obscurity" should be taken as praise since, for a poet with Tate's fine ear, the temptation, one to which he should occasionally surrender, is to write a poem of purely sonic effect and let referentiality take care of itself.

Notes

12. John Bradbury, *Renaissance in the South* (Chapel Hill: University of North Carolina Press, 1963), 30.
13. Bradbury, *Renaissance in the South*, 31.
14. "Visiting the Tates," *Prose* 60.
15. "Tension in Poetry," *Essays* 57.

—William Doreski. *The Years of Our Friendship: Robert Lowell and Allen Tate* (Jackson: University Press of Mississippi, 1990): 25–27.

Langdon Hammer on the Presence of Other Modernists

[Langdon Hammer is the author of *Hart Crane and Allen Tate: Janus-Faced Modernism* and the editor, with Brom Weber, of *O My Land, My Friends: The Selected Letters of Hart Crane* (1997). He writes on new poetry for the *New York Times Book Review*, the *Nation*, the *Yale Review*, and other magazines. His essays have also appeared in *American Literary History*, *Raritan*, and *Representations*. Here, Hammer points out the evidence, in the poem and in Tate's essays, of the impact of T.S. Eliot and Hart Crane on Tate.]

In response to Davidson's complaints about his "accusation of failure on all sides," Tate explained that the standards he brought to modern poetry were simply those of "all the poetry of the past which I have read": "My attempt is to see the present from the past, yet remain immersed in the present and committed to it. I think it is suicide to do anything else. From the attitude of my own criticism (perhaps from that of others' too!) my own poems are 'failures'" (*Davidson and Tate*, 189). This is, in fine, the argument of "Ode to the Confederate Dead"—a summary that is alert, even, to the danger of disregarding the claims of the present (or of setting up the grave in the house). But what Tate describes as measuring the poetry of the present by that of the past might be more accurately described, in the case of his own poem, as measuring the poetry of Hart Crane by that of T.S. Eliot. For in its ironization of the visionary mode, "Ode to the Confederate Dead" recapitulates Tate's identification with Eliot and his repudiation of Crane.

The ode brings these choices to the fore by its conspicuous appeals to Eliot's poetry. David Bromwich has described "Ode to the Confederate Dead" as a pastiche of Eliot's "Gerontion."[10] The ode is indeed indebted to "Gerontion" in several ways: there is Tate's rephrasing of Eliot's question ("After such knowledge, what forgiveness?"), the theme of "reconsidered passion," the wind that blows through both poems, and the dramatic monologue form. But this list, considerable as it is, only begins to suggest the ode's debts to Eliot's poetry in general. For instance, there are borrowings as unmistakable as the blind crab from "Prufrock" (and Tate's symbolic bestiary—crab, bitch, jaguar, spiders, owl, and serpent—is always used in Eliot's *manner*), and then there are borrowings whose force, if palpable, is only cumulative. Words like "nightfall," "murmur," "lean," and "whispering" do not constitute specific allusions to *The Waste Land*, but they can all be found in "What the Thunder Said." Taken together, these and other words present themselves as signs of a shared vocabulary, a collective idiom. Tate's cut-and-paste method, his oddly obvious and multiple debts to Eliot and other poets,[11] is ultimately an expression of the poem's commitment to *conformity*—or what I have called Tate's ethical commitment to received forms. On the level of style, Tate's submission to an impersonal order comes down to the imitation of Eliot.

To Crane, who in 1923 advised Tate to improve his poetry by "willfully extracting the more obvious echoes of Eliot" (Crane, *Letters*, 123), Tate's crowding of the poem with echoes of Eliot must have signified the elimination of his own presence in Tate's work. But despite all of its explicit appeals to Eliot, I would maintain that "Ode to the Confederate Dead" is unlike Eliot's poetry in ways that it is much more like Crane's. Except in the most attenuated modernist sense of these genres, for example, I doubt that Eliot ever thought of "Gerontion" as *either* an ode or an elegy. Nor can one imagine Mr. Silvero, Hakagawa, or Fraulein von Kulp, the cartoon characters in "Gerontion," turning up in Tate's poem. Being cut off from the past really *is*, for Tate's man at the gate, an experience of grief; and, in the end, this disappointment links him, in defeat, with the heroic dead, not Eliot's little old man.

It also links Tate with Crane. To say that Crane is the elegiac subject of the ode, we would have to uncover the evidence that Davidson could not when he asked, "And where, O Allen Tate, are the dead?" But Crane's presence in the ode is perceptible as "form," if not "content." Despite the ways in which Tate's poem links itself with Eliot, it never fully sounds like Eliot, because it sounds so much like Crane. For Eliot is not primarily or distinctively a pentameter poet, while Crane is, and above all in the major lyrics from the mid-1920s (poems such as "Recitative," "Possessions," "For the Marriage of Faustus and Helen," "Voyages," and "At Melville's Tomb"). Tate responded to several of those poems in draft, and he absorbed their meters in his own work—typically an iambic scheme modified by free-verse variations.[12] That metrical combination of tradition and modernity suggested to both Tate and Crane the possibility of writing a heroic modern poetry, a poetry "at once contemporary and in the grand manner" (as Tate put it in the preface to *White Buildings*). Against Eliot, the meters Tate heard in Crane's work argued that traditional forms were not in fact "dead." To align himself with Eliot, Tate had to give up that argument—which Tate did, even though he retained its formal vehicle. Crane, it has been said, tried to write a poetry like Eliot's on Whitmanian themes. Tate set himself a similarly contradictory task: to put Eliot's ideas into a poetry like Crane's. When the man at the gate mourns the dead, he is also mourning Crane.

The association in Tate's mind between Crane and the dead heroes of the ode is brought out in "Narcissus as Narcissus," an essay written six years after the suicide of the only critic of the ode whom Tate mentions. Here is fate's—and then Crane's—explication of the theme brought forward in the lines beginning, "You know who have waited by the wall":

> It is the theme of heroism, not merely moral heroism, but heroism in the grand style, elevating even death from mere physical dissolution into a formal ritual: this heroism is a formal ebullience of the human spirit in an entire society, not private, romantic illusion—something better than moral heroism, great as that may be, for moral heroism, being personal and individual, may be achieved by certain men in all ages, even ages of decadence. But the late Hart Crane's commentary, in a letter, is better than any I can make; he described the theme as the "theme of chivalry, a tradition of excess (not literally excess, rather active faith) which cannot be perpetuated in the fragmentary cosmos of today—'those desires which should be yours tomorrow,' but which, you know, will not persist nor find any way into action." (Tate, *Essays of Four Decades*, 599)[13]

Crane is introduced at this stage of the essay not simply because Tate is reluctant to tell us himself what his poem is "about" (although that is one reason); for Tate's quotation from Crane's letter also acts to renew—and remind the reader of—a friendship wholly relevant to the composition of the poem. The pathos of this renewal, of course, is that the friendship itself cannot be renewed: Tate has been cut off from his friend as emphatically and permanently as the man at the gate has been cut off from the Confederate dead. The effect is to link the dead poet and the dead soldiers, and to list, at least implicitly, Crane's own poetry of "excess" and "active faith" among "those desires which should be yours tomorrow," but which, Tate would have the reader know, "will not persist nor find any way to action."

At the same time, Tate is once again identifying himself—or, perhaps, an earlier version of himself—with Crane, who is made to speak here for a type of heroism that is inaccessible to both himself and Tate. Close to the surface of this argument, I would suggest, is an assertion that Crane himself is a model of "moral heroism," and the only sort of hero to be found in an age of decadence. (This view is explicit in the still later essay, "Crane: The Poet as Hero," as well as in Winters's late view of Crane as "a saint of the wrong religion.") Moral heroism is "personal and individual," whereas "heroism in the grand style" is impersonal and—one presumes—traditional. To choose between these kinds of heroism is to choose between romanticism and classicism, as Tate understood those terms, but there is in fact no choice to be made: Tate and his readers can at best aspire, as Crane aspired, to a moral heroism that consists in imitation—in a "private, romantic" commemoration—of epic action. If Tate diverges from Crane as much as "Ode to the Confederate Dead" diverges from "Atlantis," the difference between them is effaced in "Narcissus as Narcissus" in order to confirm what the two poets share: the belief that the modern poet should be able to write—unironically and without quotation marks—"in the grand style."

For Tate, the denial of that right produces a parable of defeat. Although, in Tate's thinking, form takes precedence over content, and the craftsman takes precedence over the visionary, form-making, as a refusal to exceed imaginative limits, finally sustains the priority of that content which is "irrecoverable." (The "buried" past Tate describes to Davidson can be construed as the "active faith" of an earlier time or an earlier self.) Form-making, as Tate sees it, is a commemorative and mimetic activity, a mode of ritual that approximates, in an age of decadence, the heroism of another era.

Although all the poems in Tate's *Collected Poems* are dated, the dates "1927/1937" at the end of the ode have a special force. (The only substantial, rather than strictly local, change Tate made after the poem's first publication was the addition of the so-called refrain—an addition that Crane thought necessary to the poem's "subjective continuity," and that Tate hoped would make the poem "seem longer than it is." The refrain is in each case a two-line, concentrated, imagistic statement, a series of variations on a theme beginning "Dazed by the wind, only the wind / The leaves flying, plunge." That such a refrain was believed to enhance the poem's continuity and make it *longer* emphasizes again the poem's competing impulses toward expansion and closure—or toward epic and lyric utterances. The refrain, by drawing, as Hollander has pointed out, on the leaves in Shelley's "West Wind" and on Hardy's revision of Shelley in "During Wind and Rain," also emphasizes the poem's ambivalent relation to romantic models: Shelley makes his way into the poem only under the aegis of Hardy—a poet Winters recommended to Tate as a suitably unsentimental antidote to romanticism.) In fine, that dating of the poem is a reminder of the *labor* of form—a labor that Tate's poem and his essay on the poem constantly emphasize. Tate's form-making insists on the poet's professional dedication to the task and on the technical expertise he brings to it. But it is also imagined as heroic work: indeed, in Tate's hands, *the duration of composition itself*, prolonged in revision, takes the place of the irrecoverable duration of the epic work. "Ode to the Confederate Dead" is Tate's terse reply to the long poems of Crane, Davidson, and others, but it is not simply a rebuttal, a refusal to engage in the same competition; rather, Tate's poem preserves, through its protracted pursuit of an "unimpugnable" form, the heroic ambition it disavows on the level of "content."

The length of time Tate worked on the ode suggests a mind turning back on itself, unable to go forward. In Tate's life, the impasse he wrote about took concrete shape in a recurrent and increasingly severe writer's block, a block which, in the 1950s, kept him from finishing the projected long poem in terza rima of which "The Swimmers," "The Buried Lake," and "The Maimed Man" are the only completed parts. The limits of poetry, as Tate came to live them, were strict indeed. Tate adjusted to those limits, in part, by turning to criticism. The end of Tate's work on the ode in 1937 coincided with the beginning of the period in which he wrote his most important literary essays. Those essays are above all writerly performances, stamped not only by Tate's expertise but by his "wit and rage." The poet-critic's work as a critic begins, it seems, only once his primary work as a poet ends.

But I would argue that Tate's criticism simply continues the intensively self-reflective project of his poetry. For form-making is a fundamentally *critical* activity, as Tate viewed this process of, in Winters's words, "evaluating" and "controlling" a given experience, and it rightly culminates in criticism. The writing of "Narcissus as Narcissus" is the final step in the process of revision, the editorial discipline of self-scrutiny, that constituted the composition of the ode to begin with. But what is most striking about this conclusion to the poem is that it is no conclusion at all. Unable, that is, to evaluate either the consequences or the origins of his poem, just as he is unable to say what his poem is "about," Tate can only say what the poem says; he can only point, with the tools of prosodic analysis, to the metrical gestures with which the form of the poem mimes its content. (The alternation between "a formal regularity" and "a broken rhythm," Tate tells us, is meant to show the maintenance and collapse of "heroic emotion" in the poem. As Tate admits, "This is 'imitative form,' which Yvor Winters deems a vice worth castigation" [Tate, *Essays of Four Decades*, 603].) In the end, even the poet-critic can do no more than renew his poem's refusal to speak.

The attitude of Tate's poetry that I characterized at the end of Chapter Three as a discourse of closure should therefore be recognized, at the same time, as a discourse of incompletion—or perhaps *de*pletion, since it is exactly the hollowness of the urn that signifies the poet-hero's transcendence, his escape from the contingencies of merely personal expression. Emptiness, the blank space of Tate's poetry, is the trophy of this Pyrrhic victory, the mark of a successful failure. When, therefore, Tate reflects, in the closing sentences of "Narcissus as Narcissus," that "there is much to be said for the original *barter* instead of *yield* in the second line, and for *Novembers* instead of *November* in line fifteen" (609), it is more than a quibble. It is a sign of how great small things have become. It is a sign of just how much the poem has left out.

Notes

10. David Bromwich, "Parody, Pastiche, and Allusion," in *Beyond the New Criticism*, ed. Hosek and Parker, 333. Bromwich, who argues on behalf of the legitimacy and value of literary imitation, is not censuring so much as categorizing Tate's poem.

11. John Hollander indicates the range and depth of allusion in Tate's poem when he points out borrowings and recastings from Stevens, Donne, Hardy, Shelley, Crane, and others—all of which, I think, can be heard as modulations in (as Hollander puts it) "the constant sound of Eliot." See Hollander, *The Figure*

of Echo: A Mode of Allusion in Milton and After (Berkeley and Los Angeles, 1981), 96–98, 121. For Tate's relations to another poet, see Jefferson Humphries, "The Cemeteries of Paul Valéry and Allen Tate: The Ghosts of Aeneas and Narcissus," *Southern Review* 20, no. 1 (1984): 54–67. Tate denied Valéry's direct influence on the ode.

12. For brief but suggestive comments on Tate's technical debts to Crane, see R. K. Meiners, *The Last Alternatives: A Study of the Works of Allen Tate* (Denver, 1963), 100–102.

13. Tate is citing a letter from Crane written sometime in early January 1927 (Crane, *Letters*, 281–83), which provides a rather detailed critique—concentrating on Tate's "obscurities"—of the draft that, presumably, Tate had also just sent to Davidson. Yet Davidson refers to "your *Elegy*" while Crane refers to "your *Ode*."

—Langdon Hammer. *Hart Crane & Allen Tate: Janus-Faced Modernism* (Princeton: Princeton University Press, 1993): 97–102.

CRITICAL ANALYSIS OF

"The Mediterranean"

The poem opens with an epigraph, altered from the *Aeneid*, which loosely translates to either "Is there a limit, great king, to our sadness?" or, mire interpretively, "What goal is made possible by our suffering," as Dupree points out in the excerpt which follows this analysis. Dupree also points out that when Tate read the poem in a series at Yale, he "corrected" the epigraph, replacing *dolorum* with *laborum*, sadness with trial. Thus, the possible implication is to question what is left after great work, or great voyage.

The question is dramatized in the poem's main juxtaposition, the journeys of the ancients against the leisure travel of the characters presented in the poem. Many critics have speculated on the meaning of that juxtaposition, and how the poem fit in with Tate's maturing ideas regarding the reconciliation of a reconstructed South and modernity with a his Agrarian ideas and staunch defense of high culture. Some opinions are included in the excerpts which follow.

The first several stanzas emphasize the place in language grand and reminiscent of Homer. Each of the first three stanzas reiterates the location, beginning with "Where we went in," before proceeding to describe the entrance or the place. The phrase carries dual meaning, indicating both where the party entered (went "in") as well as leading to their means of conveyance, "the boat," "the black hull," and "the small ship." The place is cathedral-like, geologically narrow ("slingshot wide") with high walls of "towering stone." The walls are "peaked margin of antiquity's delay," a phrase suggesting that they held a place still in time, and the party's arrival is as though back in time. The tower delays time, suspends it, holds the place nearly still, looking to the group as it must have to Aeneas. That they have gone "out of time's monotone" suggests a break from the dull procedure of years, implying some of the thrill and awe the party experiences.

Within, "no light moved," and the party's motion is portrayed as beyond their control, as a "breeze, unseen but fierce as a body loved" moves the boat, and it proceeds "onward like a willing slave." The shore, too, is "murmuring" in the next stanza, and they approach it through "seaweed" which has "parted" for them. The place is thus sensuous and seductive, so that when the party makes "feast" and has a "secret need," it is not simply for roots, but for the corporeal, even the lustful. The relation to the place, for this party, is thus bodily as well as the goal of a quest. The reader learns, later, that the goal was to "taste the famous age/ eternal here yet hidden from our eyes," and so the feast and the travel has a higher point. However, the bodily imagery of the shore and the feast suggest more visceral satisfactions as well.

That they "Devour the very plates Aeneas bore" is, as Dupree claims, a reference to the *Aeneid*, as Aeneas and his men, on arriving in Italy, ate their meals on bread, and then ate the bread. Their doing so fulfilled a prophecy given Aeneas by Helenus, son of Priam; in repeating the hero's actions and receiving the same tastes, sights, and other sensations, the experience is a communion, for the party, with the past. The fourth stanza makes it explicit:

> "Where derelict you see through the low twilight
> The green coast that you, thunder tossed, would win,
> Drop sail, and hastening to drink all night
> Eat dish and bowl to take that sweet land in!"

The party is not there to "win" a coast, but to experience. Still, they cannot quite make out the coast, the twilight is dreamlike, the sailors, then, feel "thunder tossed," and by the last two lines of the stanza, the party is fully participatory in the illusion of embodying the heroes of the epic.

The next stanza reflects on the communion. The four line essentially ask what the party had hoped to do, to fulfill, with their journey and their experience. Where they feasted, "affecting [their] day of piracy," what could such "landless wanderers" possibly get out of so specific a place? That they are landless has less to do with the fact that they sailed there than with the condition of their citizenship. The party with Tate on the day which occasioned the piece were all expatriates of one stripe or another, all people who, while some later grew to have an allegiance to a region (Tate in particular), were more citizens of the world than of a particular place. With no land left to conquer, with no frontier, with no agenda from a homeland, what rewards could place provide? What did the "ancient sea" have to show?

The reward is the "taste" of the "famous age," a sense of the intangible roots of culture, of a tradition which is, as Squires states, "Western man's." The age is "Eternal here yet hidden from our eyes," making the experience of it an act of faith. It is no wonder, then, that the communion consists of bread and wine, and that Tate, a religious poet, chose to conflate the experience of cultural underpinnings with a religious miracle. While they taste, they also sense the struggle Aeneas had as his burden when seeking a homeland, recognizing that the grapes turned into wine were a portable version of the homeland: "They, in a wineskin, bore earth's paradise."

The final three stanzas exhort the travelers to both appreciate the solemnity of their place "by the breathing side/ Of ocean, where our live forefathers sleep" and to consider their purpose. With the globe explored, carved up, conquered, and warred over many times since by the time of the party's arrival, they realize theirs is not to settle or find land, per se. "What country shall we conquer"—the speaker asks—"what fair lang/ Unman our conquest and locate our blood?" Where will they find themselves, their kin? Here, the poem begins to suggest the search for kinship is more cerebral than actual. Tate notes the history of war and senseless upheaval: "We've cracked the hemispheres with careless had!" So, then, what is one to do?

They will leave the Mediterranean, just as so many had done centuries before them, and head westward. They will not, like Aeneas, search for actual land. Rather, they will seek the ideals of homeland in the region that is theirs: "the tired land where tasseling corn,/ Fat beans, grapes sweeter than muscadine/ Rot on the vine: in that land where we were born." The images of fertility and sweetness rottened, unappreciated, unvinted, suggest they have not yet seen the land for what it is. "From the Gates of Hercules" the party will take their communion and return to see their land with new eyes, and to taste it again, and to know how its treasures, such that they are, can harbor a psychic homeland, a "culture," despite defeat, violence, and impoverishment.

CRITICAL VIEWS ON

"The Mediterranean"

GEORGE HEMPHILL ON TATE'S CHARACTERISTIC TENSION

[While describing the formal basis for Tate's use of alternating tension and relaxation in poems, Hemphill points out its specific presence in "The Mediterranean."]

The fame of Tate's essay "Tension in Poetry" (1938) has partly obscured the physical and psychological fact of tension in many of his poems. By psychological tension I mean a resistance to surrendering, developing out of an inclination to surrender, some kind of integrity. Physical tension is simply a quality of Tate's usual poetic language: "a certain unique harshness of diction and meter," as Delmore Schwartz said, "and an equally curious violence of imagery and sentiment." In the poems you find the very words *strain*, *tense*, *tension*, *taut*, *tight*, *systaltic*, and the meter is not so much crabbed as tightly wound. Hold Tate's earlier poems across the room, as it were, and the aggregate seems as taut and tense as the long elastic cord under tension that you find under the outer covering of a golf ball. "Elegy," "The Paradigm," "Ode to Fear," "Ignis Fatuus," "The Eagle," and "The Subway" all have this quality, and perhaps come under the censure of a remarkable sentence in a letter that Hart Crane wrote to Tate in 1930: "So many true things have a way of coming out all the better without the strain to sum up the universe in one impressive little pellet." Crane is criticizing a whole movement toward pure poetry. Where are the relaxed, the diastolic poems? Knowledge cannot be carried to the heart unless blood is carried there first, and the heart gets its blood by relaxing.

I do not want to compound the error of James Russell Lowell's view of Poe ("the heart somehow all squeezed out by the mind") by applying it to Tate; I am saying that this is an across-the-room view. Come closer and you find things like this, from "A Dream":

The man walked on and as if it were yesterday
Came easily to a two-barred gate
And stopped, and peering over a little way
He saw a dog-run country store fallen-in,
Deserted, but he said, "Who's there?"

Or this stanza from "Last Days of Alice":

Bright Alice! always pondering to gloze
The spoiled cruelty she had meant to say
Gazes learnedly down her airy nose
At nothing, nothing thinking all the day.

Or these lines from "The Meaning of Death":

When I was a small boy living at home
The dark came on in summer at eight o'clock
For Little Lord Fauntleroy in a perfect frock
By the alley: mother took him by the ear
To teach of the mixed modes an ancient fear.

The modes of Tate's earlier poetry are tautness and relaxation; one is glad to have both, or one for the sake of the other.

Father Hopkins said: "Nothing is so beautiful as spring." His line could never make the grade among Tate's touchstones in "Tension in Poetry"; taken by itself, the line is almost pure extension or denotation. It is a statement; but such a statement coming from a poet like Hopkins, whose native inclination is to celebrate thinginess, proves chiefly his sheer barefaced honesty, his willingness to be taken for a fool. Though Tate himself warns us in "Tension in Poetry" that "no critical insight may impute an exclusive validity to any one kind" of poetry, that essay is not as good a guide to Tate's poetry as Delmore Schwartz's essay of 1940. Schwartz showed how closely Eliot's tribute to Blake's honesty applies to Tate: "One of the essential facts about Tate's writing is the tireless effort and strained labor to be honest as a writer." His taut mode is a result of the effort to avoid the dishonest relaxation of a Stephen Vincent Benét. "It was not possible," Tate said in 1955, "that I should think Stephen Benét, an amiable and patriotic rhymester, as important as Hart Crane, an imperfect genius whose profound honesty drove him to suicide after years of debauchery had stultified his mind." In his relaxed mode, Tate follows the advice Crane himself gave him, that he should not "strain" to sum up the universe.

The bitter social criticism of the essays in verse ("Aeneas at Washington," "Retroduction to American History," "Causerie," and "Fragment of a Meditation") lies in the balance with the almost perfect ease of the final lines of "The Mediterranean":

> We've cracked the hemispheres with careless hand!
> Now, from the Gates of Hercules we flood
>
> Westward, westward till the barbarous brine
> Whelms us to the tired land where tasseling corn,
> Fat beans, grapes sweeter than muscadine
> Rot on the vine: in that land were we born.

This is almost personal, engaging, warm, but not quite; for once again the warmth is in the objects, not separable from them. After his fantastic voyage the American returns to his native country, and he can't say he loves it. But at least he understands it, and understanding may be the beginning of love. Tate's American has made the round trip, as Europeans are only beginning to do. The day of the one-way trip westward is over, and so is the day of no trip westward, the day of the mere European, who would say no doubt that we had a wasteful economy, to let such good grapes rot on the vine.

—George Hemphill. *Allen Tate* (Minneapolis: University of Minnesota Press, 1964): 20–23.

Radcliffe Squires on Tate's Intellectual "Home"

[In this essay, Squires argues that Tate's expanding sense of myth enables him to render, in his work, ideas for which mere history is inadequate.]

Four days later Tate sent Bishop a new poem, one of the best he ever wrote and one of the truly memorable poems of the entire modernist period. The circumstances immediately behind this poem, "The Mediterranean," are well documented. Shortly after settling in at Villa Les Hortensias, Allen and Caroline had gone with Ford and perhaps fifteen others on a picnic at Cassis. The picnic was held in a small cove approached through a narrow channel or *catalque* navigable only by small fishing boats. All about the shingle beach rose the dark red cliffs typical of the Riviera. The sky was utterly blue. The picnickers had a great feast. There were cocks boiled in wine and in great cauldrons a sumptuous bouillabaisse, a towering salad, a pile of cheese and fruit. An old man, known as Monsieur l'Hermite, came by foot down the cliffs, bringing the wine—sixty-one bottles. As they ate Ford remarked to Tate that it must have been in such coves that Aeneas and his band had stopped to eat. Tate bought a copy of the *Aeneid* the next day in Toulon and reread it for several weeks. In September he began to compose "The Mediterranean."[10]

The rhythmic push and drag of the poem, the repetition of words and phrases impart to "The Mediterranean" a tidal determination. At first the poem seems primarily descriptive; then in the third stanza we are told:

> And we made feast and in our secret need
> Devoured the very plates Aeneas bore.

The reference is to the *Aeneid*, Book VII lines 115–27, where Aeneas' son jokes about eating their food on slabs of bread. "We are eating our tables," he cries. Then Aeneas remembers that Anchises had prophesied that when they have so little food that they will eat the tables, their hardship is finished, they have found their new home. Tate continues upon the momentum of an ironic contrast between the opulent picnickers and Aeneas:

> Where we feasted and caroused on the sandless
> Pebbles, affecting our day of piracy,
> What prophecy of eaten plates could landless
> Wanderers fulfil by the ancient sea?

At the end he asks:

> What country shall we conquer, what fair land
> Unman our conquest and locate our blood?
> We've cracked the hemispheres with careless hand!
> . . . .
> Westward, westward till the barbarous brine
> Whelms us to the tired land where tasseling corn,
> Fat beans, grapes sweeter than muscadine
> Rot on the vine: in that land were we born.

The poem comes back—like a mind coming back from immediate pleasure to a thought that worries it—to the center of Tate's social beliefs, his uneasy Agrarianism. It comes back like a picnicker returning to his daily cares. Yet all of Tate's views have been broadened in his poem. The ancestors here are the common ancestors of Western civilization. Faceless industrialism has been converted to the westward course of empire.

In "The Mediterranean" Tate for the first time discovered a tradition in which his intellect and sensibility could make a home together. This is so because this tradition is Western man's. Similarly, Tate's "region" is for the first time fused with a universality that accommodates "tasseling corn" along with a Mediterranean cove. Later Tate would be able to employ Dante as he had Vergil to widen his vision—which is a way of saying that he learned that myth and great art would work where the simple historical sense had to fail because history itself was failing.

And, of course, Tate has his dessert; his sense of irony is satisfied in "The Mediterranean," for Aeneas' somber journey had as its aim the discovery of a new homeland, or at least the recovery of an ancestral home. Tate's picnickers have not only reversed the westward direction of civilization—but they are searching only for spiritual roots, not for land. "The Mediterranean" is the best of Tate's poems written before his fortieth year. It so completely realized itself that there was nothing much left for its twin "Aeneas at Washington." And yet Tate did not at first realize the merit of "The Mediterranean." In a letter to Bishop he passed the poem off as "not one of my best, but it has a few nice phrases."[11] Bishop's response encouraged him, and he wrote a week later about the poem then called "Picnic at Cassis": "By the way isn't Arnold's feeling for the Mediterranean nearly perfect in the last two stanzas of The Scholar Gypsy? I don't think I have anything quite that good. Perhaps the idea underlying my poem is a little more realistic—less committed to the illusion that there was ever a paradise, but my writing is not so good."[12] Soon, however, the friends to whom he had sent the poem inundated him with praise, and he later wryly observed, "I hear so many people say 'It's your best poem—so unlike your other work.'—a discouraging elegy."[13]

NOTES

10. October 6, 1932.
11. Davidson to Tate, October 3, 1938.
12. August 17, 1944.
13. January 24, 1945.

—Radcliffe Squires. *Allen Tate: A Literary Biography* (New York: Bobbs-Merrill Company, Inc., 1971): 118–120.

ROBERT S. DUPREE ON THE POEM'S SUGGESTIVE LANGUAGE

[In this excerpt, Dupree explicates which words and phrases in the poem suggest imitation of Greek and Roman texts, thereby revealing shades of meaning.]

Among Tate's highest tributes to Virgil is "The Mediterranean," after "Ode to the Confederate Dead" one of his most frequently discussed poems. The large meaning of the poem, in its exploration of the sense of history, has seldom been in doubt, and its allusions to the *Aeneid* and the original event which inspired the verses, a picnic on the shores of southern France, are well known.[14] Yet the poem continues to fascinate because of the tantalizingly suggestive resonances of its language. One dimension of the poem that has been overlooked is a possible second level of allusion beyond Virgil to a modern counterpart of

Aeneas' voyage—the colonizing of Virginia. Tate uses Michael Drayton's "To the Virginian Voyage" in his satiric "Ode: To Our Young Proconsuls of the Air" and has stressed the relevance of Drayton's poem to another satirical piece, "False Nightmare."[15] There may also be echoes of it in "The Mediterranean."

The relationship between the two poems is made plausible by certain close parallels in imagery, concept, or even sound: "Atlantis howls but is no longer steep" ("The Mediterranean") recalls

When Eolus scowles,
You need not feare,
So absolute the deepe,

from "To the Virginian Voyage."[16] Two rhyming pairs, "howl"/"scowl" and "steep"/"deep," suggest a verbal inspiration as well as a conceptual one. Furthermore, the last line of Drayton's stanza also resembles "How absolute the sea!" from "Message from Abroad." Yet another verse—"They, in a wineskin, bore earth's paradise"—reminds one of "Virginia, / Earth's onely paradise" in Drayton's poem. Virginia is the destination of the voyagers in both cases, but the New World has changed from "earth's paradise" to a "tired land" in Tate's verse. Finally, in still another passage, neglect and rot replace an effortless harvest in this "paradise,"

where tasseling corn,
Fat beans, grapes sweeter than muscadine
Rot on the vine.

Tate's unstewarded landscape reflects ironically on Drayton's cornucopia of natural goods in a land

Where nature hath in store,
Fowle, venison, and fish,
And the fruitfull'st soyle,
Without your toyle,
Three harvests more,
All greater than you wish.

The optimism of Drayton's ode, an exhortation to the voyagers as "brave heroique minds, / Worthy your countries name," is a remarkable expression of the spirit of adventure and national destiny that led the Renaissance voyagers to the New World. Tate has called it "the ignorant Edenic *enthusiasm* of Michael Drayton."[17]

At least three of Tate's poems (and possibly a fourth, "Message from Abroad") are related to Drayton's, then, and they help define one of his principal themes: the "ignorant Edenic" vision that is fixed on the "ignis fatuus" of modern utopia, the secularized version of the City of God. "The Mediterranean" opposes two poets and two voyages—Virgil's narrative of the carrying of Troy to Rome and Drayton's celebration of the new colonization of America by Europe. But the difference between them is considerable, despite the heroic cast and national fervor that Drayton tries to lend to the Virginian voyage. Both poets see their heroes as driven by the divine will, but the modern attributes an economic rather than a spiritual destiny to the venture:

> And cheerefully at sea,
> Successe you still intice
>   To get the pearle and gold,
>   And ours to hold, Virginia,
> Earth's onely paradise.

Aeneas' quest for a new home was hard and fraught with difficult decisions. Drayton's Englishmen "Let cannons roare, / Frighting the wide heaven" as though they were traveling without barriers. It is this too easy and irresponsible conquest that has led modern man to crack "the hemispheres with careless hand."

The main theme of "The Mediterranean" is the reality of place and the respect for limits. The epigraph, slightly altered from the *Aeneid*,[18] speaks of a limit (*finem*) to sorrow, but the word is ambivalent and also allows the interpretation "What goal is made possible by our suffering?" The sufferings and labors of the voyagers are meaningful because they will come to a conclusion in some permanent community. Man is limited by his sufferings, but he is also defined by them. They serve to counter his appetite, which left unchecked would devour everything. The balance between appetite and limits, between what nature offers and man truly needs, creates a proper sense of place. It is a mutual relationship between the land that man inhabits and his own spirit that leads to a respect for the character of place.

"Mediterranean" means "middle of the earth." In Tate's poem it also stands for the center of Western experience. The action that is embodied in the poem is the return to the center, the recovery of origins that gives a fresh perspective and new life to an old world. The "landless wanderers" who picnic on the coast are no longer men whose city was destroyed—they are not tied to any land at all. Their picnic is an "affectation" of a "day of piracy," not the fulfillment of a prophecy. Yet they can achieve something like Aeneas' mythical voyage in their imaginations. The opening lines of the poem echo Virgilian phrases. It is through the historical imagination that the wanderers rediscover the meaning of "antiquity's delay" and "time's monotone." Their picnic is a communion with, not simply a vision of, the past. The imagery of feasting in the poem suggests that taking "that sweet land in" is a sort of communion, even in affectation, with eucharistic meaning. The past is tasted, not simply visualized in the imagination:

> We for that time might taste the famous age
> Eternal here yet hidden from our eyes
> When lust of power undid its stuffless rage;
> They, in a wineskin, bore earth's paradise.

NOTES

14. Allen Tate, "Speculations," *Southern Review*, n.s., XIV, 226–27.

15. Allen Tate, "A Sequence of Stanzas," in *Memoirs*, 214.

16. Michael Drayton, "To the Virginian Voyage," in *The Works of Michael Drayton*, ed. John Buxton (Cambridge, Mass., 1953), 123–24.

17. Tate, "A Sequence of Stanzas," in *Memoirs*, 214.

18. Tate emends the epigraph to read correctly (*laborum* instead of *dolorum*) in the Yale Series recording *Allen Tate Reads from His Own Works* (Decca DL9130; Carillon Records YP300, 1960).

—Robert S. Dupree. *Allen Tate and the Augustinian Imagination: A Study of the Poetry* (Baton Rouge: Louisiana State University Press, 1983): 138–141.

William Doreski on Tate's Connection to Baudelaire

[While discussing Tate's value of "history and locale," Doreski shows the influence of Baudelaire on the poet.]

The source of Tate's poetic maturity is, however, not only in his choice, conscious or otherwise, of aesthetic models, but in the powerful historical sense that shapes all of his best poems. Tate was profoundly aware of the role of region, nation, and era in the making of poets and poems. His essay "The Profession of Letters in the South" demonstrates the seriousness with which he contemplated the importance of place and time in the making of literature: "Where, as in the Old South, there were high forms, but no deep realization of the spirit was achieved, we must ask questions. (The right questions: not why the South refused to believe in Progress, or why it did not experiment with 'ideas.') Was the structure of society favorable to a great literature? Suppose it to have been favorable: Was there something wrong with the intellectual life for which the social order cannot be blamed?"[7]

He was equally aware of the value of history and locale in the poem itself. "The Mediterranean," written during the European trip of 1932 and the title poem of the volume that Tate presented to Lowell in 1937, opens with a broad awareness of place and time. Its sweep of imagery subsumes both the modern and the ancient world:

Where we went in the boat was a long bay
A slingshot wide, walled in by towering stone
Peaked margin of antiquity's delay,
And we went there out of time's monotone:

Where we went in the black hull no light moved
But a gull white-winged along the feckless wave,
The breeze, unseen but fierce as a body loved,
That boat drove onward like a willing slave....

As numerous critics have pointed out, the voice of Virgil haunts this poem; Homeric phrases ("Feckless wave," "black hull") lend a powerful sense of continuity. The most striking aspect of these opening lines is the brooding sense of timelessness, as though the speaker had sailed into the past, not merely into a bay. "The Mediterranean" has something of the tone of Pound's "The Seafarer," but it is more closely linked to personal experience:

Where we feasted and caroused on the sandless
Pebbles, affecting our day of piracy,
What prophecy of eaten plates could landless
Wanderers fulfil by the ancient sea?

More centrally, "The Mediterranean" pays homage to Baudelaire in its tone, imagery, and subject; it suggests a milder rewriting of "Voyage to Cythera," replacing the ominous hanged man with a less dramatic acknowledgment of the speaker's complicity and simultaneous betrayal of the past:

What country shall we conquer, what fair land
Unman our conquest and locate our blood?
We've cracked the hemispheres with careless hand!
Now, from the Gates of Hercules we flood

Westward, westward till the barbarous brine
Whelms us to the tired land where tasseling corn,
Fat beans, grapes sweeter than muscadine
Rot on the vine: in that land were we born.

The poem is Baudelairean in inspiration rather than in calculated allusion, but the echo of the French poet's aggressive verbs and images of decay ("We've cracked the hemispheres with careless hand," "Fat beans, grapes ... / Rot on the vine") points to mutual social concerns and aesthetic empathy rather than to imitation.

Tate thought highly enough of "The Mediterranean" to place it first in his Poems 1922–1947, and it remains one of his most discussed poems, but no one has pointed out its strong structural, rhetorical, and thematic similarity to "Voyage to Cythera." Most critics dwell on the poem's classical allusions instead of its aesthetic sources. The poem may well have helped shape Lowell's approach to translation, which is a matter of free rewriting instead of conventional translation. Tate's poem is not really an "imitation" in the eighteenth-century sense; it is an original poem strongly shaped by his knowledge and love of Baudelaire, but it is similar enough to suggest that "Voyage to Cythera" was on his mind. He did claim, at least in one instance, to have rewritten a Baudelaire poem. In his late essay "Translation or Imitation?" he argued that "Death of Little Boys" evolved from a translation of Rimbaud's "Le chercheuses de poux."[8]

NOTES

7. "The Profession of Letters in the South," *Essays* 523.
8. "Translation or Imitation?" *Memoirs* 199.

—William Doreski. *The Years of Our Friendship: Robert Lowell and Allen Tate* (Jackson: University Press of Mississippi, 1990): 18–20.

CRITICAL ANALYSIS OF

"Aeneas at Washington"

Aeneas' story was a powerful one to Tate, and to a number of Southern writers, due to its themes of defeat and the quest for redemption and renewal as well as the tragic posture of its hero. "Aeneas at Washington" is only one of several Tate poems to include allusions or mentions of the hero, and many feel it is not a particularly strong example. But critics suggest it is the one "Aeneas poem" most often discussed (aside from "Ode to the Confederate Dead") because it appears in the *Collected Poems* immediately following an acknowledged masterpiece, "The Mediterranean," and it shares the same general theme.

The poem opens with a stunning image of awareness, of the hero seeing himself "furious with blood," having witnessed the savagery of Neoptalamus' felling of Priam while his queen, Hecuba, and his hundred daughters suffered. The blood of Priam stanches flames: "his filth drenching the holy fires." The reference could be to the actual burning of Troy, but given the adjective "holy," it could also be pyres. Aeneas, duly impassive in his understatement, says, "In that extremity, I bore me well/ A true gentleman, valorous in arms,/ Disinterested and honourable." Aeneas is both moved and impassive, a paradox Tate thought could be readily understood by the Southern mind, by a people defeated, psychically destroyed by that defeat, and yet proudly desirous of not *appearing* defeated to the enemy. To reveal the degree of suffering would have been, to Aeneas as well as to Tate's mythical Southerner, ignominious.

But Aeneas has the benefit of flight, whereas those living in the South and having supported it do not have the benefit. The Aeneas story thus has attracts and fascinates Tate. After the reader learns of Aenea's dispassionate façade, he flees. As the hero states, "That was a time when civilization/ Run by the few fell to the many, and/ Crashed to the shout of me, the clang of arms." What might sound like the goal of populist uprising or democracy is instead portrayed by the poet as a mob, something from which the hero must escape. After the wise elite had been ruling, the war cast "civilization" into disorder by putting civilization in the hands of the many. Aeneas leaves the bedlam and, "in the smoke" or out of the disarray and veils of a sort, emerges from darkness to make "by sea for a new world." He brings little with him. The stanza ends with Aeneas's suggestion that he brings only his mind, his ideals. He brings no "things;" to do so would be to cling to the "tenuous." His comparison of sentimentality or nostalgia is to "receding love." Both ultimately fade, but this hero has them fixed in the mind. The result is Tate once again making memory and the past the motivation of a hero.

Aeneas' motivation, then, is to rebuild Troy. The next stanza, a parenthetical, is a direct reference to the construction of Washington, and the fact that it was and is a city designed and built upon themes and concepts rather than migration, community, and trade. In this poem, Aeneas participated in the building of Washington. "Littorals" are coastal areas, often swampy or marshy, and so the poet writes, "To the reduction of uncitied littorals/ We brought chiefly the vigor of prophecy,/ Our hunger breeding calculation/ And fixed triumphs." He describes how the "vigor of prophecy," that is, the certainty of success and goals, actually filled the swamp so that men might build. The "reduction of uncitied littorals" is the production of coastal metropolises. Thus, Aeneas' arrival is characterized by "hunger," "prophecy," and "calculation." The hero is urgent and determined, desirous and filled with the memory of his homeland.

In the third stanza, he again remembers Troy. The previous stanza is parenthetical because, for Aeneas, Washington is really secondary to Troy. He wants Troy, wants to build Troy again, but even his ideas on building and his complicity in erecting a nation's hollow city do nothing to diminish the memory of Troy. The third stanza uses familiar imagery: he sees "the thirsty dove," a sign of peace that cannot find peace, "In the glowing fields of Troy." The fields glow with plenty, and with flora native to Tate's own remembered home, Kentucky: "hemp ripening," "tawny corn," "thickening Blue Grass," and the "green sun." The image is of late summer, of harvest and abundance. The images are, also, things, importantly substantive, reflecting a place built on the things unique to it.

But his vision now, of Washington in particular and men in general, is full of remembrance and experience, and is bitter for it. He sees, in the buildings of Washington, the effects of contrivance: "the towers that men/ Contrive I too contrived long, long ago." He has also seen them fall. So, he says, "Now I demand little. The singular passion/ Abides it object and consumes desire/ In the circling shadow of its appetite." He realizes that passion consumes, that appetite is our undoing. Aeneas, here, is ancient, and has seen enough cycles to know. Later, when he makes reference to the ninth buried city, it is implied that he has seen them all become buried.

The lines which follow have Aeneas tell of "a time when the young eyes were slow," when they were lit from a "flame steady beyond the firstling fire." He tells of his own eyes, but the implication is of many viewers, of a larger sense of people. He remembers looking at Washington as he "stood in the rain, far from home at nightfall/ By the Potomac." The top of the Capitol, "the great Dome," is reflected in the river, it "lit the water." It is reflection and light, nothing like the substance (the Kentucky substance) comprising the riches of Troy. Tate's Agrarian ideals are at work here. Troy was of a place, whereas Washington was built on an idea. In the case of Aeneas, the idea of Troy informed Washington, and so the city is only a fading copy, a perversion of it. In a larger sense, Tate looks at the Yankee capital as one built on the premise of ancient ideals but which is, in fact, hollow, unresponsive to the very things which comprise the land and people for which it stands.

Aeneas, looking at the city he helped make, realizes that "The city my blood had built I knew no more." He hears a screech-owl, then, a symbol both of death and of Athenian wisdom, and a hunter cloaked in the dark. His "new delight" could be at any of the frustrations and alienation of Aeneas.

The poem closes with Aeneas reconsidering his place and his role. He is "Stuck in the wet mire/ Four thousand leagues from the ninth buried city." He is away from his home, standing in the mud, in the earth that is not firm beneath. This city, we can infer, will also become buried. He then thinks of Troy, "what we had built her for." Because he thinks of the reasons for building, he could be thinking of the actual Troy, or of Washington. His questioning of the reasons is the weight of the poem. Now that Aeneas has lost and suffered, has traveled and built, has revered his memory and worshipped his past, he has made something intangible and false. The questions Tate asks through Aeneas are: what are the costs of memory when it drives us? What is the effect of building the future on defeat?

CRITICAL VIEWS ON

"Aeneas at Washington"

RADCLIFFE SQUIRES ON TATE'S PAIRS OF POEMS

[In a concluding portion of the biography, and after analyzing Tate's last published poem, "The Buried Lake," Squires shows how pairs of poems characterize Tate's treatment of certain themes and ideas, usually with one being stronger than the other. In this context, he includes "Aeneas at Washington," and goes on to make broad statements about Tate's aim as a poet.]

With these confident lines Tate's published poetry ceases. Looking at the three late poems one sees that they belong to a pattern repeated throughout Tate's career. It is a pattern in which we are conscious of a ratio of relative failures to relative successes. "The Maimed Man," fine as it is in places, fragments, and the macabre elements will not stay with the rational. "The Buried Lake" *vibrates* continuously but does not *move* very far. "The Swimmers," perfectly attuned to Dante's form, moves through its journey-encounters and stands at last, as all fine poetry does, not as a set of symbols, but as an action which is in toto symbolic. Now, this same ratio may be observed in the summits of all of Tate's poetry. "Ode to the Confederate Dead" emerges from a context of several inferior poems that are thematically similar. "The Mediterranean" rises above the lesser poem "Aeneas at Washington"; "Seasons of the Soul" issues from the lesser poem "Winter Mask." But that is only part of the pattern. It remains to be observed that all of these poems are concerned with integrity or its absence. The visitor to the Confederate graveyard is locked in his sensibility; the picnicker at the Mediterranean cove has exchanged the telic search of Aeneas for a search for those spiritual roots which will give him a sense of wholeness; the man who looks at World War II and perceives that the world is a dead land, perceives also that the world could be restored by love—although he is not sure that love can be found; the man who sinks into the buried lake of the self is self-baptized, and his pastoral vision is restored. Tate was right, then, when he told his friends that he was always writing only one poem. But there are peaks in the one poem and these peaks obtained with the most severe effort throughout his career are the poems which make him one of the masters of a varied and brilliant epoch. But even if his superior poems had not come, he would still be an important poet, for we should have "Death of Little Boys" instead of "Ode to the Confederate Dead." We should have "The Buried Lake" instead of "The Swimmers." And we should pay them homage as examples of a poetry that strained, indeed wrenched, the language with bitter zeal. We should see, moreover, that that zeal was one that sprang from a refusal to tolerate falseness either in the self or in man in general. Tate's language is of that kind which wells forth when the poet presses with all his force for a victory which he knows he will not obtain.

Because he has been unable to lie to us about victory, his poems have never been very popular. For popular poetry is the kind that encourages people who are not poets to believe that they are. Tate's poetry cannot have that effect. But the effect it can and does have is that of reminding us that the heroic, the saintly act is a subjective—even a hidden—act of such private intensity that its public implementation is only an inevitable step, not a greater step. In this way Tate is entirely different from T.S. Eliot whom he resembles in such obvious but superficial ways that some critics stopped digging for the treasure when they found a few coins in the topsoil. Eliot's poetry has no private morality. His figures are either public saints or paralyzed puppets, just as his cats are either practical or dead. But it is by reason of this very difference that Tate in his later poetry could achieve an optimism that never came to Eliot. One can after all save what can be saved if he does not try to save what cannot be saved.

—Radcliffe Squires. *Allen Tate: A Literary Biography* (New York: Bobbs-Merrill Company Inc., 1971): 211–213.

Robert S. Dupree on the Poem's Imaginative Leap

[Dupree outlines Tate's speculation on what Aeneas would think on perceiving Washington and, in doing so claims that Tate's poem critiques the hubris of such a city.]

In contrast to the Virgilian fable of the refounding of Troy is the modern exploration of the universe for its own sake. The Gates of Hercules were the natural limits beyond which the Greek world felt it should not venture. But now that "We've cracked the hemispheres with careless hand," there is no longer a sense of time and place in our experience. Reality is no longer accessible to man unaided by his mediating technology. Places are no longer a "slingshot" or "a month" wide. They are mere abstract points on a map, neither fearful nor impressive. Only in the imagination can we return to the state of things that characterized Virgil's world, but that return to the remembered center is of primary importance:

> Let us lie down once more by the breathing side
> Of Ocean, where our live forefathers sleep
> As if the Known Sea still were a month wide—
> Atlantis howls but is no longer steep!

The unknown no longer frightens modern man, but he has lost the power of keeping his known world alive. Only through the remembered image of all cities, mythical or real, can he know how to settle down and foster his own.

This symbolic stratification of cities is the focus of Tate's companion piece, "Aeneas at Washington," usually printed after "The Mediterranean." It reverses the situation of the first poem. Instead of dramatizing the discovery by a modern American of the scenes where the Trojans might have landed, Tate imagines Aeneas discovering the shores where the Americans have landed and settled, carrying his Rome to other shores. Aeneas speaks and compares his own actions during the fall of Troy with the motives of the men who have made Washington what it is; he looks back on his flight from the burning city without self-recrimination:

In that extremity I bore me well,
A true gentleman, valorous in arms,
Disinterested and honourable.

After he has done all that can be achieved for his stricken city, Aeneas turns to those things that matter to him personally—his wife and the "old man" his father—and leaves for a new world after taking up "cold victualing" (for eating also has a great prominence in this poem). But the crisis is not simply a matter of foreign invasion; there has been an internal change as well: "civilization / Run by the few" has fallen "to the many." Aeneas knows that only two things can survive the collapse of a civilization: "a mind imperishable" and "a love of past things." Aeneas hastily gathers up the few definite things about him—the household gods (his *prima sacramenti memoria*)—and hoists his father, symbol of the living past, onto his back. All that remains of the particular Troy he was a part of is his love of it, "tenuous as the hesitation of receding love" symbolized by the fading ghost of his first wife Creusa.

Although Aeneas is aware of the divine origins of his conquering energies, he recognizes that his chief responsibility lies in exercising them with prudence and restraint.

(To the reduction of uncitied littorals
We brought chiefly the vigor of prophecy,
Our hunger breeding calculation
And fixed triumphs.)

The words that play against each other are all Latin-derived—"reduction" is tempered by "vigor," "calculation" by "fixed." The behavior common to ravaging conquerors has been muted and softened. The point of the aside is that any human community is a matter of compromise between good and bad elements, but exaggerated Latinisms like "littorals" also remind the reader that "reduction" (*reductio*, a "leading back") and "calculation" have neutral senses. Aeneas, like other men, has lust for power, but he has learned to control and contain it because he has the knowledge of his city's destiny that will limit his ambitions. In fact, Aeneas alone possesses the controlling detachment that is possible when life is informed by a myth; he can "see all things apart." The proper human proportion of desire is, after all, related to reasonable fulfillment. There is no lust for power in Aeneas' meditations:

> Now I demand little. The singular passion
> Abides its object and consumes desire
> In the circling shadow of its appetite.

Unlike the modern explorer or pioneer, Aeneas can be satisfied because his desire does not stray from its object and is eliminated once his appetite is satisfied.

What Aeneas sees, however, has certainly been swollen out of proportion to the needs of refounding a fallen city. Looking at Washington, the first city in the world created specifically for government, Aeneas must admit that his original motives for building a new community have become unrecognizable: "The city my blood had built I knew no more." Washington is a city built not with blood but with geometric abstractions and disembodied ideas. Washington is the symbol of what Spengler calls "infinite relations, conceivable only in pure Space" by the Faustian imagination. The Greeks, according to Spengler and others,[19] abhorred the "desensualized idea of infinity of the Unextended," or "Time actualized as infinite Space." The great dome of the Capitol is a new symbolic center of the universe, but the light that plays about it suggests the enlightenment of the abstract will for power rather than a return to a traditional cosmos, and this city of Faustian men has been created through the imposition of a geometric pattern on the "wet mire" of the world. Aeneas finds himself at an enormous distance from "the ninth buried city" of his homeland, and his alienation is created by a disjunction of both time and space.

The darkest image in the poem, however, is the screech-owl's whistle, a sound that in "Ode to the Confederate Dead" evokes the fury of battle. In this poem it may represent another allusion to the *Aeneid*. The owl is, of course, Athena's bird and a symbol of wisdom; but in oriental and middle-eastern mythologies, it symbolizes "death, night, cold and passivity," according to J.E. Cirlot. Since confronting the dark and coming to a deeper understanding are not opposed in Tate's other writings, it may be that the owl stands for both. Cirlot says that the owl symbol "pertains to the realm of the dead sun, that is, of the sun which has set below the horizon and which is crossing the lake or sea of darkness."[20] Associated with twilight, the owl can be seen as the harbinger of Spengler's final phase of civilization. Certainly Tate uses it as an image of falling time and twilight:

> I stood in the rain, far from home at nightfall
>
> While the screech-owl whistled his new delight
> Consecutively dark.

But even more suggestive is the Virgilian parallel that occurs toward the end of the *Aeneid*, when Megaera in the form of an owl causes Turnus to recognize the inevitability of his fate:

> She beholds the Trojan armies and the troops of Turnus, having suddenly contracted into the form of the little bird, which sometimes sitting by night on graves, or abandoned roofs, untimely sings her late strain among the shades.[21]

The sight of the dome and all its pretensions to permanence is challenged by the sound of the bird; once again Tate opposes the visual and the aural to suggest transience.

NOTES

19. Oswald Spengler, *The Decline of the West*, trans. Charles Francis Atkinson (New York, 1939), I, 67–73; F.M. Cornford, "The Invention of Space," in *Essays in Honour of Gilbert Murray* (London, 1936), 215–35.

20. J.E. Cirlot, *A Dictionary of Symbols*, trans. Jack Sage (New York, 1962), 235–36.

21. Virgil, *The Aeneid*, XII, 874–80 (my translation).

—Robert S. Dupree. *Allen Tate and the Augustinian Imagination: A Study of the Poetry* (Baton Rouge: Louisiana State University Press, 1983): 142–145.

Elsa Nettels on the Poem's Agrarian Statement

[Elsa Nettels is Professor Emeritus of English at the College of William and Mary. Her books include *James and Conrad*; *Language, Race, and Social Class in Howells's America*; and *Language and Gender in American Fiction: Howells, James, Wharton, and Cather*. Here, Nettels considers the poem as a source for Cather and points out that the Aeneas in Tate's poem is stuck in memory, to the point of an inability to act.]

In the works of Cather and Tate, the *Aeneid* most *fully* informs "Tom Outland's Story" and "Aeneas at Washington" (1933) [11] — texts that illustrate Cather's affinities with and fundamental differences from the Southern Agrarians. In both poem and novel, the speaker, imbued with Aeneas's sense of a heroic past, confronts in Washington the corruptions of the modern city and dwells upon his sense of isolation and alienation amid people consumed by their struggle for wealth and power. In neither poem nor novel does the speaker imagine reform or even express hope for change.

At the end of his narration in book 2 of *The Professor's House*, Tom Outland recalls his journey from the Mesa to Washington, where he hoped to persuade the director of the Smithsonian to send archaeologists to the Mesa to complete the work of excavation begun by Tom and Roddy Blake. Soon he learns that money rules actions in official Washington: he can gain access to the director only by buying his secretary an expensive lunch; instead of funding an expedition to the Mesa, the director and his staff will seek lavish expense accounts and lucrative appointments at an exposition in Paris. Tom not only fails in his mission but becomes increasingly depressed in the city by the sight of "hundreds of little black-coated men pouring out of white buildings" (235), slaves of the bureaucracy, all struggling to make more money, to secure invitations and make connections, all living beyond their means in order to keep up appearances. "They seemed to me like people in slavery, who ought to be free" (232). Measuring worth by money, the Bixbys, from whom Tom rents a room, speculate about the salaries and promotions of co-workers, as preoccupied with material possessions as St. Peter's family.

In Tate's poem, the speaker Aeneas remembers himself as he stood on the shores of the Potomac, where "the great Dome lit the water," fusing in one symbol the cities of ancient Rome and Washington. He reveals the soulless materialism of the modern city indirectly, by dwelling upon all that has been lost of his heroic past. "Far from home at nightfall," he recalls the fall of Troy and his own conduct in battle and defeat.

> In that extremity I bore me well,
> A true gentleman, valorous in arms,
> Disinterested and honourable.

In the destruction of his city he sees the collapse of social order.

> That was a time when civilization
> Run by the few fell to the many, and
> Crashed to the shout of men, the clang of arms.

His arduous journey to the "uncitied littorals" where he was destined to found a new state has ended in the modern capital, where the "vigor of prophecy" has lapsed in "fixed triumphs" of leaders ruled by appetite.

Like heroic virtue, the fruitful land exists only in memory. He imagines "the glowing fields of Troy," reminiscent of the poet's native Kentucky, filled with

> hemp ripening
> And tawny corn, the thickening Blue Grass
> All lying rich forever in the green sun.

Thus Aeneas realizes the magnitude of his loss, not only of his homeland but of the ideal city he would found:

> The city my blood had built I knew no more
> While the screech-owl whistled his new delight
> Consecutively dark.

Struck in the wet mire
Four thousand leagues from the ninth buried city
I thought of Troy, what we had built her for.

In Tate's poem, it is not difficult to read the lament of the southerner who mourns a lost homeland devastated by war, like Troy, and sees in the defeat of the Confederacy the passing of the "true gentleman, valorous in arms." Tate's speaker dwells not upon the destiny of Aeneas to found a new state but upon the defeated city recoverable only in memory. "Struck in the mire," he cannot go forward, but moves ever deeper into the past, beyond defeat in war to the founding of his city.

Like the lost world of Troy evoked by Tate's speaker, the Pueblo ruins discovered by Cather's Tom Outland signify an agrarian society, according to Guy Reynolds, "the organic, agrarian community beloved of American pastoral idealists from Jefferson through to the Fugitives" (140). But unlike Tate's speaker, Tom Outland moves forward to a transforming vision of the past that "brought with it great happiness" (249). He suffers the anguish of loss when he returns from Washington to the Mesa and learns that Roddy Blake has sold all the Indian artifacts to a German dealer for four thousand dollars. But the loss of the material objects enables Tom to gain what is more precious than pottery and turquoise. Alone on the Mesa, he is not, like Tate's speaker, "far from home," but he comes at last into possession of his spiritual home. On the Mesa, where he reads and memorizes long passages of the *Aeneid*, he gains his heritage, which inspires in him the "filial piety" (249) memorialized in the poetry of Vergil. Every morning, he recalls, "I wakened with the feeling that I had found everything, instead of having lost everything" (250). He looks to the future, not the past, and does not return for the diary he had hidden before going to Washington. "It would have been going backward. I didn't want to go back and unravel things step by step" (250).

Of all Cather's characters, St. Peter in some ways most resembles the speaker of "Aeneas at Washington." Tate's figure portrays himself as an old man, his life of action long over, his ambition dead.

I see all things apart, the towers that men
Contrive I too contrived long, long ago.
Now I demand little. The singular passion
Abides its object and consumes desire
In the circling shadow of its appetite.

These could be the words of St. Peter, who looks back on his life as scholar, teacher, husband, and father as if it no longer belonged to him. "It seemed to him like the life of another person" (265). For him, as for Tate's Aeneas, the desire to strive, to build towers, seems dead, like the fire consumed by its ashes. As Aeneas recalls his youth "when the young eyes were slow, / Their flame steady beyond the firstling fire," so St. Peter recovers the reality of his solitary elemental childhood self, even as he dwells upon death, feeling himself "near the conclusion of his life" (266).

St. Peter's memories of Tom Outland—of their friendship, their conversations, their travels to the Southwest—are to him what memories of his homeland are to Tate's Aeneas—the most poignant and precious of life-giving images. But Tate's speaker remains transfixed by memory, which by itself can effect no spiritual change. St. Peter's refusal to leave his attic study, symbolic of his bitter resistance to change, nearly costs him his life when the gas from his rusty stove overpowers him. But the accident does what his will could not do—it frees him from the pain of futile longing for the irrecoverable. "His temporary release from consciousness seemed to have been beneficial. He had let something go—and it was gone: something very precious, that he could not consciously have relinquished, probably" (281). At the end, he is "outward bound" (280), prepared to live "with fortitude" if not with passion and delight, and the final words of the novel are "the future" (281).

NOTE

11. Tate 68–69.

—Elsa Nettels. "Aeneas and *The Professor's House.*" *Willa Cather's Southern Connections: New Essays on Cather and the South*, ed. Ann Romines (Charlottesville: University Press of Virginia, 2000): 175–178.

CRITICAL ANALYSIS OF

"The Swimmers"

In one of the excerpts which follows, Thomas A. Underwood shows that the autobiographical genesis of this poem came from Tate's remembering, four decades afterward, a lynching of a black man that had occurred in his town in Montgomery County, Kentucky. The poem's occasion and sentiment cause many who read and defend Tate to cite it as an example that, while Tate was a reluctant and slow-to-come-around supporter of integration in the South, he was not a flinty racist as were so many of his contemporaries.

The narrative poem is entirely in *terza rima*, the formal procedure of the poem a stark contrast to the chaos it describes. It is also a parody; *terza rima* is a structure historically employed for elegy or heroic tales. At the same time, the form gives the poem the momentum and style to skirt the meat of the horror in the same way that the town itself did not acknowledge or recognize the horror in their midst, something for which the poem indicts them. Finally, the poem's structure delivers episodes, with turns roughly every four stanzas, giving it the feel of sequential poems, marching portions which guide through the story.

The poem's first line carries a situation of threat. We see "A boy fleeing" to the water with his friends. The next stanza sets the scene further; while the first stanza was water and clarity, the second is already growing with "Long shadows," cast by grapevines, a symbol of fertility. The boys, four of them, run toward the water, "Over the green swirl; mullein under the ear/ Soft as Nausicaä's palm." Mullein, a medicinal American herb with hairy leaves, grows wild throughout the country, and would have been known to locals as an indigenous and useful herb. Nausicaä is a Phaeacian princess who, on discovering the shipwrecked Odysseus, directs him to the castle of her father, Alcinous, who arranges to return Odysseus to Ithaca. The overtones, thus, are of safety and return to home, of the water as both a comfort and, with the overtone of Odysseus, a potential peril.

Tate was exceptionally well-schooled in classical tales and their significance, so the inclusion of both classical references and local fauna would have been entirely intentional and a powerful combination of the worldly and the regional, a critical tenet to Tate's particular Agrarian philosophy. The combination of comfort and threat are underscored again with the oxymoron following: "sullen fun// Savage as childhood's thin harmonious tear." Tate adds savagery to the sense of the moment, and invokes a tear, again, in unexpected description. By the end of the third stanza, the water, spring-fed, is both "undying-dead" and a "spring of love and fear," and the fourth stanza has the speaker, in the present, asking to have returned to him the "eye that looked and fled," that witnessed and backed off, or recoiled. He is, essentially, recalling a moment of lost innocence and complex complicity.

The moment features a "thrush"—a scarcely seen woodland bird with a song prized by birders—"idling in the tulip tree" which announced, or "unwound" the "cold dream of the copperhead." The bird is a thing of beauty and evasiveness, and the copperhead is lurking and treachery, and with the tulip tree, the three images are a sort of trinity for the region. Odysseus is invoked again in the fifth stanza, as Tate's speaker remembers the companions with him, and the names suggest an idyll, being children, and also, with the presence of "'Nigger Layne," an acceptance, albeit not an elegant one by today's standards. As Underwood reveals, Tate's inclusion of "water on the brain" is a signal of the poet's actual presence in the work, and a remembered joke.

Tate sets the time, "Dog-days," and shows the leaves "dusty," and the only plants at this pointing the poem are "poison-oak and scuppernong," one an irritant, the other a smaller, more bitter grape common to the American South. The wilderness, in a way, is closing, tightening, becoming more mean. The shade is "active"—thus moving, creeping, perhaps, but is also "Of water." The boys head toward it, can hear it.

But as they hear the water, which "bells and bickers" at night, they also hear hooves, in the next stanza, the ninth. The posse numbers twelve, and the leader's face "Was worn as limestone on an ancient sill." His face is the stone of grave markers, and he is ancient; Tate's treatment is mythic, and so the tragedy is underscored here. The boys, after hearing the posse pass, "scuttle" down the bank to march in "common fright" near the stream. They march, in their descent—a descent which recalls the descent of so many gods and heroes in various trials—and enter a world "where sound shaded the sight," where they can hear what transpires, but cannot see it. The poem itself works the way the town's knowledge of the lynching works. The reader hears about it, knows it is happening, but does not seem to acknowledge.

The leader has stayed behind, and night settles by the next stanza. Tate's speaker "feared: eleven same/ Jesus-Christers unmembered and unmade,/ Whose Corpse had died again in dirty shame." On their way out, the Jesus-Christers are no longer a unity of purpose, and they now number eleven (all but one apostle, perhaps), and Tate's point is that they have crucified again, in shame, the god they claim to serve. The rhythm and rhyme of the *terza rima* give the line a bludgeoning, near-righteous force.

In their absence, the bank levels, the boys are in a "speckled glade," a place of rest in the American artistic and literary imagination. They stop to "breathe," and the shade, "reticulated" now, like netting, is invoked again in the same stanza, reinforcing both the quiet and the menace. In the stanze that follows, the fear Tate's speaker feels is given the trappings of submersion, as though drowning. The fear is "blue," and it rolls over him, lifts his hair "like seaweed tossing on a sunk atoll," or a lost land. Tate's speaker rises, and on the copper air (the color recalling the copperhead of an earlier stanza), a voice "green as a funeral wreath/ Against a grave" points out the dead black man.

The sheriff, beneath a sycamore, realizes he is too late. The poem suggests he is neither pleased nor sorry; he picks his teeth with sassafras, but also shakes his head. In the woods, the sheriff is enveloped by the natural surroundings. His immersion echoes that of the boys' at the beginning of the poem. As the wilderness moves toward them and surrounds them, so too does it surround the sheriff. However, as in the example of the "butting horse fly," the sheriff is not only terrorized by the forest's increasing malevolence, he encounters it as well, in the form of the body, the horror in the midst of, and thus *part* of, the forest. The dead man, described as "tired" to show his trials, is still in a ragged shirt which has soaked up the blood. The sheriff, again a mix of reactions, kicks the noose away from the man's neck.

At that point, Tate's speaker looks up and sees his friends had gone. A single horseman arrives, the sheriff's help, and the sheriff loops the rope—the same one which had hanged him—around the dead man's "horny feet." The indignities of the corpse mount, even in Tate's descriptions. The comparison of the dead man's straightening to a fish line which "Yields to the current that it must subtend" is Tate speaking of the current of violence that has swept all of the town's citizens into a broad culpability, which will be revisited in the final stanza.

The sheriff curses, as Tate points out, "Not for the dead but for the blinding dust." The poet then transforms the dragged man and the horse into a procession, a "cortege," which then moves toward town. As it departs, the speaker realizes he cannot stay on the road, especially after dark, for fear of the return of the posse, or worse. He runs over the ground, the "stonecrop"—a low-growing and long living creeping plant, and he does so like a toad, reifying the link between the speaker, the dead man, the posse, and the natural environs. He follows the body into town, where before the courthouse it is deposited, the "corpse that took the sun for a shroud"—a death shroud of light, a contradiction as powerful as the juxtaposition of the forested glade witnessing a lynching death. The three figures—an unholy trinity of sorts—are so powerful a presence of wrong in the square that the "dying sun" shone a light that "were company where three was crowd."

The speaker's breath is loud in the quiet, crackling "the dead air like a shotgun." The officials disappear. Viewing the "faceless head," the speaker cannot move. His final lines implicate the town, the region, the place, and are perfectly clear as they do so: "This private thing was owned by all the town,/ Though never claimed by us within my hearing."

CRITICAL VIEWS ON

"The Swimmers"

RADCLIFFE SQUIRES ON TATE'S FORMAL APPROACH

[In this extract, Squires describes the effect of the poem's form in a larger discussion of the poems grouped with it, "The Maimed Man" and "The Buried Lake," two other of Tate's poems often discussed by critics.]

"The Swimmers" did exactly what Tate hoped it would. The terza rima worked perfectly. The imagery presented thematic epiphanies. Furthermore, the poem is so lucid that any extended "interpretation" would constitute an insult. "The Swimmers" retells, with only a few facts altered, the experience Tate had of seeing when he was eleven the body of a lynched Negro dragged into the town of Mount Sterling, Kentucky. The lynching was not the standard "rape-case." The Negro had murdered his landlord after an altercation, but Tate does not specify any background to the lynching, for he wants the drama to remain a universal agony upon which he can affix his personal yet conforming specifics. There are visible specifics—even the names of his playmates are given. He goes so far as to make a joke at his own expense. His memory of his parents' apprehension that he suffered from hydrocephalus appears in his reference to "Tate, with water on his brain." A compound joke, philosophical, religious, as well as biographical.

The ending of "The Swimmers" is true to the important fact of the incident—the town never admitted to itself that the lynching had occurred:

My breath crackled the dead air like a shotgun
  As, sheriff and the stranger disappearing,
  The faceless head lay still. I could not run

Or walk, but stood. Alone in the public clearing
  This private thing was owned by all the town,
  Though never claimed by us within my hearing.

Unimportant facts were changed for dramatic purposes. Tate did not, as in the poem, follow the sheriff back into town, but cut through the fields and beat him into town. Nor, in the actual incident, did Tate's companions desert him. But the solitariness of the boy who followed the "cloudy hearse" was necessary to the full impact of the Jesus-Christers' ritual sacrifice of the Negro. The town itself had to be rendered as nearly deserted as possible so as to tune to a blinding sharpness the focus upon all humanity's desolation in evil. In that desolation we perceive that the evil must be "owned."

Robert Lowell wrote to Tate to say that "The Swimmers" was the best poem Allen had ever done, the finest terza rima in English. He found it better even than Shelley's use of the form.[3]

NOTE

3. March 15, 1954.

—Radcliffe Squires. *Allen Tate: A Literary Biography* (New York: Bobbs-Merrill Company, Inc., 1971): 206–207.

ROBERT S. DUPREE ON THE POEM'S NARRATIVE AND SYMBOLISM

[In this excerpt, Dupree discusses the symbolism and meaning in the poem's story and images.]

It is not altogether certain that Tate intended "The Maimed Man" to be followed immediately by "The Swimmers," but a transition at the end of the first poem seems to point directly to the second. The references to water, for instance, are amplified in "The Swimmers." In this poem, the actions of diving and "witching for water" are given specificity by a recalled incident from the poet's memory, and the movement of the poem as a whole has the same pattern of discovery, peripety, and recognition that characterize its predecessor. Again a young man is plunged into a terrifying experience. Once more there is a succession of dawns and twilights. Even the country setting of "The Swimmers" appears to be anticipated by the "Pastoral terrors of youth" described in "The Maimed Man." But the difference between the two poems is considerable. Both are about "maimed" men; but the first poem describes a dream experience, while the second takes its main scenes from an actual event in the life of the poet. Because it has a more readily discernible story to tell, "The Swimmers" has tended to attract the kind of reader who prefers straightforward, easily accessible narrative.

The poem is an evocation of the freewheeling pleasures of boyhood. During the "dog-days" of Kentucky summer, the speaker and his childhood companions go out in search of water. Theirs is an "odyssey" where, if they cannot expect to meet a real Nausicaä, the natural world of mullein and grapevine is almost as enticing as a girl's hand. But before Odysseus was washed ashore on the coast of a fairyland Phaiakia, he underwent many trials; and the fun these boys experience is not altogether idyllic. The poet describes it as "sullen" and "savage as childhood's thin harmonious tear." Once again Tate seems to be alluding to "Lycidas" ("He must not float upon his watery bier ... without the meed of some melodious tear"), reminding one that water is traditionally associated with death and sorrow as well as with birth and joy. The innocence of the "sleek senses" must yield to the more discriminating power of the mature eye:

> O fountain, bosom source undying-dead
> Replenish me the spring of love and fear
>
> And give me back the eye that looked and fled
> When a thrush idling in the tulip tree
> Unwound the cold dream of the copperhead.

In "The Swimmers" the opposition between laurel and myrtle is altered to a complementarity. The thrush and the copperhead, love and fear, the "undying-dead" fountain with its systaltic rhythm, the carefree and the didactic are all at the "bosom source" of the heart, mortal and immortal. The plunge into the water is both an escape from the summer's blast and an acceptance of the drowning sea. Is the fountain to be understood as *memoria*, the "clear springs," or the "harmonious tear" or all of them? The feeling of alienation from community and from the depths of the self is not as important in this poem as it is in "The Maimed Man." "The Swimmers" is about the larger dimensions of guilt and alienation that a whole community discovers in itself. The poet's memory returns him to an incident he witnessed in which the City of Man and the City of God, like the other oppositions disclosed by Tate's poetic dialectic, intersect in a specific time and place.[1]

As the "shrill companions" appear now in the eye of memory (rather than in the eye of the ego), they take on symbolic overtones. The rich descriptive language that chronicles their walk along a creek road under a clear, hot sky moves from a visual to an auditory emphasis. There is a delight in the music of words that was absent from "The Maimed Man." The catalog of heroes, five boys whose real names are given, may have no intended significance, but it is interesting that two besides Tate are identified by more than their names. One is a doctor's son and the other is a flautist. Medicine and music are also complementary arts, one for healing the body and another for soothing the soul. They are also traditionally associated with Apollo, their patron. Tate, the lad who even then was "maimed" before his time "with water on the brain," is obsessed by the need for water (and redemption); he is already the "dull critter of enormous head" from "Sonnets at Christmas" who looks at the sky in search of transcendence. It is amusing that he has these Apollonian figures in his entourage.

The increasing predominance of sounds over sights points to some impending revelation. As the boys follow the "bells and bickers" of the noisy waters, they hear another sound, which seems "at first a song" but turns out to be horses' hooves. Like the thrush who revealed the snake, these sounds are soon followed by a posse and sheriff, whose face is as worn as a tombstone. The mood shifts abruptly. Day suddenly seems night;

the reality, a nightmare. The boys walk into a world on the edge of fear, "where sound shaded the sight." Seeing yields to hearing, but when sight returns, the boys discover the sheriff leaning over the dead body of a lynched Negro. The boy Tate never gets a chance to swim, but he is plunged immediately into a drowning fear:

> We stopped to breathe above the swimming hole;
> I gazed at its reticulated shade
>
> Recoiling in blue fear, and felt it roll
> Over my ears and eyes and lift my hair
> Like seaweed tossing on a sun atoll.

When he regains his bearings, the boy hears only two phrases: "That dead nigger there," and "We come too late." As he watches the men, the boy notes both the sheriff's casualness in the face of death and his reluctance to touch the body, his regret for what has happened and his scant respect for the dead man. The sheriff removes the rope from the hanged man's neck with his foot and attaches it to the feet. The body is drawn forward, like a Hector pulled around the walls of Troy; yet the ignominious treatment of the body seems to flow from embarrassment or even fear, rather than hatred. The dead man, brought to dust, is made to advertise his earthly destiny prominently as the body is dragged to town "boxed ... in a cloudy hearse" and taking only "the sun for shroud." The event occurs in broad daylight, though the sun will soon begin to set. The eleven "Jesus-Christers" of the posse abandon the scene "unmembered and unmade" like the fearful apostles who abandoned Jesus; they fail to see the significance of the "dirty shame" that they have witnessed. Yet the "three figures in the dying sun" are an emblem that the poet in retrospect sees as a kind of new Calvary.

Tate's daring evocation of crucifixion imagery is made convincing by the incidental details, like the sheriff's unintended irony in uttering "Goddamn" or the "butting horse-fly" that pauses on the ear of the corpse. There are no accusations, no moral heroes, and no villains in the scene. Even the argument that led up to the lynching is ignored as irrelevant. The terrible scene has been witnessed by "all the town." Lynching is another form of the scapegoat ritual, as René Girard has shown,[2] a means of attempting to restore order by going beyond established order in the name of the sacred. Like original sin, the responsibility for what has happened must be shared equally by all in the community:

> Alone in the public clearing
> This private thing was owned by all the town,
> Though never claimed by us within my hearing.

The community has not given its sanction for the execution nor expressed publicly its regret for what has happened. The event lies rather on the borderline between universal guilt and universal responsibility that cannot be articulated without diminishing its impact.

In a remarkable simile, Tate describes the dead body when it is first pulled forward:

> I saw the Negro's body bend
> And straighten, as a fish-line cast transverse
> Yields to the current that it must subtend.

Though the Negro has been lynched, not drowned, the comparison is rich in implications, for it connects his death with the feeling of helplessness that overcomes the boy when he first sees the awesome sight. The behavior of the fishline, like the dead body, manifests both a yielding and a resistance that are like the desperate plight of the lynched man. The tug of the rope is a crucifixion of sorts, but it also seems to merge the body with some larger force beyond it. The body is now part of the greater current of an anonymous natural power that sweeps all things before it. The "faceless head" of the body makes the death appear both terribly impersonal and yet symbolically particularized. The boy who has never managed to go swimming and the dead man whose body swims only in simile have merged. The faceless death's head that the boy encounters upon emerging from his plunge is a grim counterpart of the dead mother's face that was the object of his dive in "The Maimed Man." The maimed man that the poet discovered within himself in the first poem has now merged with the hanged god of Frazer. Memory has disclosed the identity of fear with love, guilt with transcendence. In recognizing that he is guilty, man acknowledges that he is imperfect and incomplete. That acknowledgment is the confessional act that opens the mind to an awareness of its need for some transcending power beyond it, a dimension that can restore wholeness to the self and deliver it from alienation and dissociation.

Notes

1. Allen Tate, "Speculations," *Southern Review*, n.s., XIV, 232.
2. René Girard, *Violence and the Sacred*, trans. Patrick Gregory (Baltimore, 1977).

—Robert S. Dupree. *Allen Tate and the Augustinian Imagination: A Study of the Poetry* (Baton Rouge: Louisiana State University Press, 1983): 219–223.

William Doreski on Tate's Breaking New Ground

[In this portion of the essay, Doreski compares the poets' use of child personae (using Tate's "The Swimmers" as an example) and focuses on how each poet covers the new ground in their work.]

The headless figure of "The Maimed Man," as Robert Dupree argues, is "the symbol of the passive remnant of a once flourishing people."[35] It is a figure projected by the speaker's psyche, generated by his willingness to see the whole of Christian and pagan mythology brought to bear on the cultural present. As such, it is not merely the maimed representative of the antebellum South but of all civilization worthy of the name. This figure recurs in specifically southern terms as the hanged, mutilated black man of "The Swimmers," where it occasions the loss of innocence and the assumption of both individual and communal guilt on the part of the speaker, here a mere child. Once fully materialized and integrated within the speaker's psyche (as the embodiment of guilt, for Tate a necessary, natural emotion), the figure need not reappear in "The Buried Lake." This poem struggles to regain a vision in which guilt is not expunged for the speaker but is incorporated into a fallen, though still beautiful, natural world.

The identity of the various figures in the trilogy has caused critics some anguish, but granting them various roles resolves the apparent complexity of function. Like the lady in *Ash Wednesday*, they change as the speaker changes, and since their function is symbolic, they can maintain multiple identities. St. Lucy, for example, in "The Buried Lake," is the patron saint of music, the muse of poetry, the representative of the Virgin Mary, and the icon of human love. But the speaker himself is multiple in nature. In "The Maimed Man," he assumes a representative role; in "The Swimmers," he plays a specifically autobiographical role; and in "The Buried Lake," he resumes the stance of representative persona.

Both the representative suffering individual and the autobiographically specific self attain a psychological and aesthetic depth that is new to Tate's work, and this revamping of the speaker's role sets an example for Lowell. The representative sufferer easily shifts roles from epic voice to human witness:

> Then, timeless Muse, reverse my time; unfreeze
>   All that I was in your congenial heat;
>   Tune me in recollection to appease
>
> The hour when, as I sauntered down our street,
>   I saw a young man there, headless, whose hand
>   Hung limp; it dangled at his hidden feet....

This confrontation with what becomes a form of alter ego recurs in Lowell's work, most notably in "The Severed Head." As R.K. Meiners argues, "This confrontation with the alter ego has been obsessive with both men."[36] Lowell had learned from Tate how to dramatize that alter ego and how to give voice to a persona that can incorporate it into his consciousness. Meiners is correct in arguing that the superficial resemblances between the poems of Tate and Lowell mean little; it is the dealing with a dramatic confrontation with disparate aspects of the self that links the two poets here. This example did not necessarily make it possible for Lowell to write "The Severed Head," "Skunk Hour," and other poems in which the speaker feels that the constriction of his world is focusing him upon some distorted or maimed aspect of himself, but it did encourage him by the example of self-confrontation that Lowell praises in the opening of his 5 November letter.

The child persona of "The Swimmers" is more dramatically presented than the child persona of "My Last Afternoon with Uncle Devereaux Winslow" or "Dunbarton," but both function primarily as witness, secondarily in their willingness or need to assume the burden of what they have seen. "The Swimmers" uses an evocative summer setting to contrast with the cruelty of the unfolding drama, one in which the child has no direct part. "My Last Afternoon with Uncle Devereaux Winslow" does the same. Both narrators are passive, unable to fully comprehend what they witness, yet instinctly alert to its significance. Each child-narrator is more sensuously aware of the earth than of the dramatic horror unfolding before him:

> I knew I must
> Not stay till twilight in that silent road;
> Sliding my bare feet into the warm crust,
>
> I hopped the stonecrop like a panting toad
> Mouth open, following the heaving cloud
> That floated to the court-house square its load
>
> Of limber corpse.... ("The Swimmers")

> Our farmer was cementing a root-house under the hill.
> One of my hands was cool on a pile
> of black earth, the other warm on a pile of lime.
> ("My Last Afternoon with Uncle Devereaux Winslow")

In neither case is the child indifferent to the death that, in Tate's poem, has actually occurred or, in Lowell's, is forthcoming. Rather, as a child, he is limited in his options, forced by his immaturity into the role of bystander. Tate's child confronts the possibility of assuming a communal guilt and realizes the difficulty of admitting to the perceived crime:

> Alone in the public clearing
> This private thing was owned by all the town,
> though never claimed by us within my hearing.

Lowell's child-persona expresses his meager understanding of death in appropriate and sensuous imagery derived from a world already familiar to him [*Lowell's ellipsis*]:

> My hands were warm, then cool, on the piles
> of earth and lime,
> a black pile and a white pile....
> Come winter,
> Uncle Devereaux would blend to the one color.

Characteristically, Lowell's poem is more concrete and sensuous and creates the more convincing atmosphere, the stricter evocation of the child's point of view.

We might wonder, along with Meiners, what these resemblances and differences prove. Lowell is not merely imitating Tate. He became a poet under the mentorship of Tate, and his attachment to the elder poet is not merely personal; it is the relationship that Harold Bloom has so well described between the strong precursor poet and the ephebe who sets himself the task of rewriting—not merely imitating—the precursor's work. The relationship is more complicated, though, because after *Lord Weary's Castle*, Lowell is the stronger poet. When Tate comes to realize this, and realizes that, by the late 1950s, his own poetic career is complete, he rebels against the reversal of roles. Confronted with Lowell's most revisionary poetry—that of *Life Studies*—he simply declares the younger poet mad again. Still later though, perhaps realizing the importance of his own role in Lowell's success, Tate will reconcile himself to becoming the elder statesman and will show more critical flexibility in dealing with Lowell's further shifts of style.

NOTES

35. Robert S. Dupree, *Allen Tate and the Augustan Imagination* (Baton Rouge: Louisiana State University Press, 1983), 215.
36. R. K. Meiners, *Everything to Be Endured: An Essay on Robert Lowell and Modern Poetry* (Columbia: University of Missouri Press, 1970), 32.

—William Doreski. *The Years of Our Friendship: Robert Lowell and Allen Tate* (Jackson: University Press of Mississippi, 1990): 100–103.

THOMAS A. UNDERWOOD ON TATE'S SOCIAL THINKING

[Thomas A. Underwood teaches Expository Writing at Harvard University and is a frequent lecturer on Southern history and literature, he has also taught at Columbia, Boston, and Yale universities. In this excerpt, Underwood considers the poem in light of Tate's evolving views on segregation and integration in the late 1940s and early 1950s.]

Tate found opposition to neither his segregationist nor his paternalistic race attitudes among Agrarian comrades such as Robert Penn Warren, who often made equally disturbing statements. After Mabry accepted a job at all-black Fisk University, for instance, Warren wrote to say that "Mabry has definitely decided to commercialize his talent for nigger-loving."[176] When Warren wrote his segregationist essay for *I'll Take My Stand* in 1930, Tate praised his friend's ideas, which he believed were in the best interests of blacks. Warren's "views of negro education," Tate told Davidson, "seem to me to be sound: if we don't educate the negro into a self-sufficient agrarianism, the industrialist will propagandize him into the factory.... The salvation of the negro lies in sticking to the land."[177]

If Tate shared Warren's halfhearted interest in the education and economic plight of Southern blacks, he believed such aid was endangered by Northern reformers challenging the Southern race hierarchy.[178] When it came to his disdain for these reformers, Tate's views on race relations during the Agrarian period were indistinguishable from those of the fire-eating Agrarian, Frank Owsley. Like Owsley's, Tate's remarks about race issues were often accompanied by attacks against "Eastern liberals" and Communists. The Agrarians, Tate argued in the early 1930s, might have been able to join forces with radical writers when they protested labor conditions in Harlan, Kentucky, but in a case such as the Scottsboro trial, the Nashville group's views on race relations would make it impossible. "Not because," he wrote the Harvard-trained John Brooks Wheelwright, "the nine, or is it ten, colored boys are guilty, or if not guilty ought to be hanged anyhow, but because the unfortunate negro, when your compatriots paid us a four year visit in the last century, was turned over to the mercies of the poor white mob. It has always been an impossible situation, and there's nothing we can do short of presenting the negro agitators with the case they most desire: defense of ten negroes would be defense of the whole race. Rather than that, I will shut my eyes, and see the colored boys executed. You have no idea what it is to live—and not merely sympathize from Boston or New York—with another race; and for that and all the complicating reasons I see the negro question in terms of power. When there are two unassimilable races one of them must rule; and being white I prefer white rule, and I will not give up the slightest instrument of white rule that seems necessary. It's too bad that the negro has no interested protector—for example, an owner—and is at the mercy of the mob. I see no solution."[179]

Flickers of a pained conscience did occasionally appear in poetry Tate wrote during the Agrarian movement. The African American poet and anthologist Arna Bontemps recognized that, even in the 1930s, when Tate wrote *Sonnets at Christmas*, he was ashamed of his behavior toward blacks.[180] "Ah, Christ, I love you rings to the wild sky," the second sonnet began.

And I must think a little of the past:
When I was ten I told a stinking lie
That got a black boy whipped ....
Therefore with idle hands and head I sit
In late December before the fire's daze
Punished by crimes of which I would be quit.[181]

But such confessional moments in Tate's poetry, or elsewhere, were rare during the 1930s. Indeed, his views on race issues, as well as his belief in segregation, remained relatively unchanged through the 1940s. He would make no public amendments to his views until the 1950s, by which time his expatriation from the South—and a long series of charges that he was undemocratic—made him more self-conscious about his social pronouncements.[182]

Tate startled many critics by writing, in 1950, an introduction to the poetry of Melvin Tolson that Tolson called the "literary Emancipation Proclamation" for black American writers.[183] Readers who had a view of Tate as an unreconstructed Southerner were equally surprised when they read his terza rima poem *The Swimmers*. Written after he experienced a flashback, in 1951, to the sight of a lynched man he had come upon in Kentucky some forty years earlier, Tate recalled seeing the "limber corpse" and pondered the actions of his townsmen. "Alone in the public clearing," he wrote in the poem's final stanza, "This private thing was owned by all the town, / Though never claimed by us within my hearing."[184]

Before the 1950s were over, Tate participated in a two-day civil rights forum titled "The Sectional Crisis of Our Time." Martin Luther King delivered the keynote address and Tate's lecture, given on the same day—the centennial of the raid on Harper's Ferry—consisted of an attack against the radical abolitionist John Brown. Tate told the audience he would rather adopt "a more recent strategy—the example of Dr. Martin Luther King, whose leadership in the non-violent resistance of his people in the now famous boycott of the bus system in Montgomery is to my mind a model of the kind of action that should be undertaken all over this country." Tate called King's model "an imperfect one, not inherently imperfect, but rather incomplete" and appeared to be supporting integration for reasons of practicality as much as for anything else. "The political and social welfare of all Americans," Tate said, "and not only justice to the Southern Negro, demands that the Negro everywhere be given first-class citizenship."[185]

Tate's support of voting rights for African Americans and his begrudging endorsement of integration was accompanied by a growing impatience with the segregationist tirades of his more conservative friends like Davidson, who joined the White Citizens Council at Vanderbilt during the 1960s. Davidson's "Southernism," Tate complained to Robert Penn Warren, "for all its cunning and learning, is now at the level of mere White Supremacy."[186] Yet Tate remained a gradualist who preferred that integration, which he supported largely because it was inevitable, be overseen by Southerners.[187] "If you can't lick 'em, join 'em, might well be the Southern slogan," he wrote Davidson; "that is, take over integration and do it gradually the Southern way."[188]

Once Martin Luther King's movement began to triumph, however, Tate found it difficult to maintain any loyalty to Southern diehards such as Davidson. For a while, Tate tried to walk a tightrope between his Southern and Northern friends. He told Anthony Hecht that blacks might have gained their civil rights without so much difficulty had they delayed their early push for educational integration, which he believed had "aroused the deepest prejudices of ... the ignorant Southerner."[189] Praising King's voter registration drive as a more practical starting point, Tate perhaps thought he had found a way to support the campaign for civil rights without endorsing integration across-the-board.

Yet the more Tate observed the actions of those Southerners violently opposed to King's movement—and the nation's horrified response to them—the more self-conscious he became. Finally, he seized an opportunity to publicly disassociate himself from the Southern segregationists. Writing for the *Spectator* on April 9, 1965, the anniversary of the confederate surrender at Appomattox, he denounced the segregationist governors George Wallace and Ross Barnett—as well as the "half literate Red

Necks" at sporting events who were unfurling the Confederate flag. "An elegiac devotion to the Confederate flag," he argued, "can have a dignified propriety. There is no dignity in displaying it as a symbol of the oppression of the Negro. It once stood for the best of the South; it now stands for the worst." He had seen the flag "diminished to a small emblem set in the helmets of the Alabama State Troopers" who appeared "on television beating Negroes, who were trying to register to vote, with clubs, wet ropes, and cattle prods." Although Tate continued to express cynicism about the chances for producing social equality in the South by educating people, he restated his belief that "the vote is the fundamental political reality, from which other liberties must come or not at all."[190] He was proud of having veered away from neo-Confederates such as Davidson and told Robert Penn Warren (who was undergoing a political conversion of sorts and publishing more liberal, while no less paternalistic, work on Southern race relations) that his piece on Appomattox was "a personal confession which might have been subtitled 'Up from Segregation.'"[191]

NOTES

176. Warren to Tate, fragment [ca. 1931], AT–PU, 44:28.

177. Tate to Davidson, 22 July 1930, DD–VU. Both Davidson and Lyle Lanier thought Warren's essay too liberal! See Davidson to Tate, 21 July 1930, AT–PU, 18:2; Lanier to Tate, 1 Aug. 1930, AT–PU, 27:8. For a Southern liberal's reaction to the treatment of race issues in *ITMS*, see Ralph McGill, *The South and the Southerner* (1959; repr. Boston, 1964), 82.

178. See Tate to Lytle, 2 June 1933, TDY–L, 82–84, 83.

179. Tate to John Brooks Wheelwright, 25 Feb. 1932, JBW–BRN. Tate attempted to conflate such white supremacist thinking and Agrarian paternalism in his review essay, "A View of the Whole South," *American Review* 2 (Feb. 1934): 411–32, 423–25, 426.

180. Arna Bontemps to Langston Hughes, 10 November 1966, in *Arna Bontemps–Langston Hughes Letters, 1925–1967*, ed. Charles H. Nichols (New York, 1980), 477.

181. Tate, *Sonnets at Christmas, Collected Poems*, 103. Tate explained to Anthony Hecht: "I told a lie to escape punishment that got a negro playmate of mine punished, and I didn't have the courage to confess the he.... [A]t the age of 65 I am still rather haunted by that occasionally. Because this boy Henry was about a year older than I am and he was drafted in the first World War and he was killed in Japan, I never had a chance to apologize to him" (Tate–Hecht, 34).

182. During World War II, Tate continued to harbor hostility toward Northern race reformers. In 1943, for instance, he wrote a letter to the governor of Tennessee in which he urged "responsible Southern leaders" to take action lest "irresponsible and ignorant people in the North" begin to "take over the leadership of the negro." Along with the letter, in which he defended segregation, Tate forwarded some literature he had received in the mail, describing it to Cooper as "the most recent specimen of Eastern racial agitation." The literature, Tate told the governor, was "well within the historic pattern of abolitionist feeling, an attitude that may be defined as the desire to improve the morals of people at a distance with no cost to oneself" (Tate to Gov. Prentice Cooper, 17 Sept. 1943 [carbon copy, unsigned: "fc/at"] AT–PU, AM 19629, 16:13). In Tate's wartime correspondence with Frank Owsley and Donald Davidson, he also expressed agreement with the race attitudes of the two most reactionary Agrarians. (See Tate to Owsley, 18 Nov. 1943, FO–VU; Tate to Davidson, 4 Aug. 1944, 13 Oct. 1944, & 27 Jan. 1945—all in DD–VU; and Davidson's segregationist diatribe, "Preface to Decision," in the *Sewanee Review* 53 [July–Sept. 1945]: 394–412, written at the request of, and privately praised by, Tate, who was then editing that journal.) When Tate published a partly critical editorial responding to Davidson's article, he warned that "any responsible leader who ignores Mr. Davidson's central argument ignores it at the peril of the south and the country." ("Mr. Davidson and the Race Problem," *Sewanee Review* 53 [Oct.–Dec. 1945]: 659–60, 660.) Nevertheless, Tate simultaneously professed to hold more moderate and pragmatic views than Davidson, with whom he expressed impatience and some disagreement when writing to other friends (see Tate to Brainard Cheney, 18 Oct. 1945, BC–VU; and Tate to F.O. Matthiessen, 16 Oct. 1945, Yale Collection of American Literature, Beinecke Rare Book and Ms. Library, Yale University).

Coley has written of the postwar Tate, "As a citizen of a wider world, Tate felt, I think, that southern racism and the exploitation of blacks made him and his intellectual position vulnerable. I think he wanted to somehow ease the situation of blacks without altering the structure of southern society, not a rare stance for educated southerners before the Civil Rights movement. Over the years he made gestures that later seemed patronizing or fainthearted to some, such as his foreword to Melvin B. Tolson's *Libretto for the Republic of Liberia*; but they meant something to him" ("Memories and Opinions of Allen Tate," 954).

183. Tolson to Tate, 15 March 1950, AT–PU, AM 19629, 42:21.

184. Tate, "Speculations," *Southern Review* 14 (April 1978): 226–32, 232; *The Swimmers*, *Collected Poems*, 132–35, 135. Of this final line, Coley observes, "Tate closed the poem with a home truth most southern writers couldn't manage." Such authors, Coley adds, "presented racial terrorism as the work of cranks and rednecks, people marginal to the community" ("Memories and Opinions of Allen Tate," 955).

185. Program, "American Studies Conference on Civil Rights" (photocopy courtesy of Mrs. Lucy Bowron); Tate, untitled typescript of speech delivered at the University of Minnesota, 16 Oct. 1959, 6 pp., with corrections in Tate's hand (photocopy courtesy of Mr. Paul Collinge, Heartwood Books, Charlottesville, Va.), 2, 4.

186. Tate to Warren, 5 Oct. 1960, RPW–YU. See also Tate to Lytle, 9 Sept. 1959, TDY–L, 284, and Dan Ross, "Memories of Allen Tate," 13 March 1980, 15-page typescript, 4–5.

187. See Tate to Jesse Wills, 18 May 1962, JW–VU; Tate to Davidson, 19 Oct. 1962, DD–VU; Tate–Hecht, 38–40, 38.

188. Tate to Davidson, 23 Nov. 1962, DD–VU.

189. Tate–Hecht, 38–40, 38.

190. Tate, "April 9,1865: *A Peroration a Hundred Years After*," 5-page typescript, AT–PU, 3:6. See also "Appomattox, April 9, 1865: A Peroration a Hundred Years After," *Spectator* (April 1965): 467–68.

191. Referring to Warren's *Who Speaks for the Negro?* (New York, 1965), Tate wrote, "Your general point of view I share completely, and I hope it will have some effect on Negro leadership as well as upon white people, North and South." Tate to Warren, 8 June 1965, RPW–YU.

—Thomas A. Underwood. *Allen Tate: Orphan of the South* (Princeton: Princeton University Press, 2000): 292–295.

WORKS BY

Allen Tate

Mr. Pope, and Other Poems, New York: Minton Balch, 1928.

Stonewall Jackson: The Good Soldier: A Narrative, New York: Minton Balch, 1928.

Ed. (with others) *Fugitives: An Anthology of Verse*, New York: Harcourt, Brace, 1928.

Jefferson Davis: His Rise and Fall: A Biographical Narrative, New York: Minton Balch, 1929.

(With others) *The Critique of Humanism*, New York: Harcourt, Brace, and Company, 1930.

(With others) *I'll Take My Stand: The South and the Agrarian Tradition by Twelve Southerners*, New York: Harper, 1930.

Poems: 1928–1931, New York: Scribner, 1932.

The Mediterranean and Other Poems, New York: Alcestis Press, 1936.

Ed. (with Herbert Agar) *Who Owns America?: A New Declaration of Independence*, Boston: Houghton Mifflin, 1936.

Reactionary Essays on Poetry and Ideas, New York: Scribner, 1936.

Selected Poems, New York: Scribner, 1937.

Ed. (with A. Theodore Johnson) *America through the Essay: An Anthology for English Courses*, New York: Oxford University Press, 1938.

The Fathers, New York: Putnam, 1938.

(With Huntington Cairns and Mark Van Doren) *Invitation to Learning*, New York: Random House, 1941.

Sonnets at Christmas, Cummington: Cummington Press, 1941.

Reason in Madness: Critical Essays, New York: Putnam, 1941.

Ed. *The Language of Poetry*, Princeton: Princeton University Press, 1942.

Ed. *Princeton Verse between Two Wars: An Anthology*, Princeton: Princeton University Press, 1942.

Ed. (with John Peale Bishop) *American Harvest: Twenty Years of Creative Writing in the United States*, New York: Garden City Publishing, 1942.

Recent American Poetry and Poetic Criticism: A Selected List of References, Washington, D.C.: Library of Congress, 1943.

(Translator) Pervigilium Veneris, *Vigil of Venus*, Cummington: Cummington Press, 1943.

The Winter Sea, Cummington: Cummington Press, 1944.

Ed. *Sixty American Poets, 1896–1944*, New York: Morrow, 1945, revised edition, 1954.

Fragment of a Meditation/MCMXXVIII, Cummington: Cummington Press 1947.

Ed. *A Southern Vanguard: The John Peale Bishop Memorial Volume*, New York: Prentice-Hall, 1947.

On the Limits of Poetry: Selected Essays, 1928–1948, New York: Swallow Press, 1948.

Ed. *The Collected Poems of John Peale Bishop*, New York: Scribner, 1948.

Poems: 1922–1947, New York: Scribner, 1948; enlarged edition, 1960.

The Hovering Fly and Other Essays, Cummington: Cummington Press, 1948.

Ed. (with Caroline Gordon) *The House of Fiction: An Anthology of the Short Story*, New York: Scribner, 1950, revised edition, 1960.

The Forlorn Demon: Didactic and Critical Essays, Chicago: Regnery, 1953.

The Man of Letters in the Modern World: Selected Essays, 1928–1955, New York: Meridian Books, 1955.

Ed. (with David Cecil) *Modern Verse in English, 1900-1950*, London: Jarrold, 1958.

Collected Essays, Denver: A. Swallow, 1959; revised and enlarged as *Essays of Four Decades*, Chicago: Swallow Press, 1968.

Ed. (with John Berryman and Ralph Ross) *The Arts of Reading*, New York: Crowell, 1960.

Poems, New York: Scribner, 1960.

Ed. (with Philip Wheelwright and others) *The Language of Poetry*, New York: Russell and Russell (New York, NY), 1960.

Ed. *Selected Poems of John Peale Bishop*, New York: Scribner, 1960.

Christ and the Unicorn: An Address, Cummington: Cummington Press, 1966.

Ed. *T.S. Eliot: The Man and His Work: A Critical Evaluation by Twenty-six Distinguished Writers*, New York: Delacorte, 1967.

Mere Literature and the Lost Traveller, Chicago: Swallow Press, 1968.

Ed. *Complete Poetry and Selected Criticism of Edgar Allan Poe*, New York: New American Library, 1968.

The Swimmers and Other Selected Poems, New York: Scribner, 1971.

Ed. *Six American Poets from Emily Dickinson to the Present: An Introduction*, Minneapolis: University of Minnesota Press, 1971.

The Translation of Poetry, Washington, D.C.: Library of Congress, 1972.

Memoirs and Opinions, 1926–1974, Chicago: Swallow Press, 1975.

Collected Poems, 1919–1976, New York: Farrar, Straus, 1977.

The Fathers and Other Fiction, Baton Rouge: Louisiana State University Press, 1977.

WORKS ABOUT

Allen Tate

Allen, Walter. *The Modern Novel: In Britain and the United States*, New York: Dutton, 1965.

————. *Allen Tate: A Recollection*, Baton Rouge: Louisiana State University Press, 1988.

Allums, J. Larry, *Tate and the Poetic*, Baton Rouge: Louisiana State University Press, 1984.

Arnold, Willard Burdett. *The Social Ideas of Allen Tate*. Boston: Bruce Humphries, 1955.

Binding, Paul. "Above the Abyss: Allen Tate and the Old South," *The Times Literary Supplement* 5042 (November 19, 1999): p. 14.

Bishop, Ferman. *Allen Tate*. New York: Twayne Publishers, 1967.

Brinkmeyer, Robert H. *Three Catholic Writers of the Modern South*. Jackson: University Press of Mississippi, 1985.

Bradbury, John M., *The Fugitives: A Critical Account*, Chapel Hill: University of North Carolina Press, 1958.

Bradford, M. E., *Rumors of Mortality: An Introduction to Allen Tate*, Dallas: Argus Academic Press, 1969.

Brown, Ashley and Frances Neel Cheney, eds. *The Poetry Reviews of Allen Tate: 1924–1944*, Baton Rouge: Louisiana State University Press, 1983.

Bruce, Cicero. "The Stand of Allen Tate," *Modern Age* 42:4 (Fall 2000): p. 331–45.

Buffington, Robert. "A Conservative Revolution?" *The Sewanee Review* 110: 3 (Summer 2002): p. 471–7.

Burt, Stephen. "Rebellious Authority: Robert Lowell and Milton at Midcentury," *Journal of Modern Literature* 24:2 (Winter 2000/2001): p. 337–47.

Carrithers, Gale H. *Mumford, Tate, Eiseley: Watchers in the Night*. Baton Rouge: Louisiana State University Press, 1991.

Chappell, Fred. "'Not as a leaf': Southern Poetry and the

Innovation of Tradition," *The Georgia Review* 51 (Fall 1997): p. 477–89.

Coley, Lem. "'A Conspiracy of Friendliness': T.S. Eliot, Ezra Pound, Allen Tate, and the Bollingen Controversy," *The Southern Review* 38:4 (Autumn 2002): p. 809-26.

———. "Memories and Opinions of Allen Tate," *The Southern Review* 28 (Autumn 1992): 944–64.

Cowan, Louise, *The Fugitive Group: A Literary History*, Baton Rouge: Louisiana State University Press, 1959.

Deutsch, Babette, *Poetry in Our Time*, New York: Holt, 1952.

Doreski, William. *The Years of Our Friendship: Robert Lowell and Allen Tate*. Jackson: University Press of Mississippi, 1990.

———. "Founding a Literary Friendship: Allen Tate and Robert Lowell," *The Southern Literary Journal* 22(21) (Spring 1989): p. 72–91.

Dunaway, John M., editor. *Exiles and Fugitives: The Letters of Jacques and Raeissa Maritain, Allen Tate, and Caroline Gordon*, Baton Rouge: Louisiana State University Press, 1992.

Dupree, Robert S. *Allen Tate and the Augustinian Imagination: A Study of the Poetry*. Baton Rouge: Louisiana State University Press, 1983.

Edwards, Margaret F. "An Explication of Allen Tate's 'Ode to the Confederate Dead,'" *Contemporary Poetry* 1:1 (1973): p. 31–4.

Fain, John Tyree and Thomas Daniel Young, eds. *The Literary Correspondence of Donald Davidson and Allen Tate*, Athens: University of Georgia Press, 1974.

Fallwell, Marshall, Jr., *Allen Tate: A Bibliography*, New York: David Lewis, 1969.

Faulkner, Steven. "Two Mid-Century Critics," *Modern Age* 45:1 (Winter 2003): p. 85–91.

Foster, Richard, *The New Romantics: A Reappraisal of the New Criticism*, Bloomington: Indiana University Press, 1962.

Frye, Northrop, *Northrop Frye on Culture and Literature: A Collection of Review Essays*, Chicago: University of Chicago Press, 1978.

Grammer, John M. "Reconstructing Southern Literature," *American Literary History* 13:1 (Spring 2001): p. 126–40.

———. "Fairly Agrarian," *The Mississippi Quarterly* 52:1 (Winter 1998/1999): p. 143–8.

Hammer, Langdon. "The American Poetry of Thom Gunn and Geoffrey Hill," *Contemporary Literature* 43:4 (Winter 2002): p. 644–66.

———. "Caroline Gordon, Allen Tate, and Hart Crane: An Exchange." *The Sewanee Review* 106:1 (Winter 1998): p. 140–5.

———. *Hart Crane & Allen Tate: Janus-Faced Modernism.* Princeton: Princeton University Press, 1993.

Hearon, Todd. "Corpse in the Kitchen, Poem in the Hole," *Partisan Review* 70:1 (Winter 2003): p. 154–9.

Hemphill, George. *Allen Tate.* Minneapolis: University of Minnesota Press, 1964.

Huff, Peter A. *Allen Tate and the Catholic Revival: Trace of the Fugitive Gods.* New York: Paulist Press, 1996.

Humphries, Jefferson. "The Cemeteries of Allen Tate and Paul Valery: The Ghosts of Aeneas and Narcissus," *The Southern Review* 20 (January 1984): p. 54–67.

Hux, Samuel. "For Mr. Tate," *Modern Age* 36 (Winter 1994): p. 150–6.

Jancovich, Mark. *The Cultural Politics of the New Criticism.* New York: Cambridge University Press, 1993.

Kazin, Alfred, *On Native Grounds: An Interpretation of Modern American Prose Literature*, Reynal & Hitchcock, 1942.

Kingsley, Lawrence. "The Texts of Allen Tate's 'Ode to the Confederate Dead'," *Papers of the Bibliographical Society of America* 71 (1977): p. 171–89.

Malvasi, Mark G. *The Unregenerate South: The Agrarian Thought of John Crowe Ransom, Allen Tate, and Donald Davidson.* Baton Rouge: Louisiana State University Press, 1997.

Meiners, R.K. "The Art of Allen Tate: A Reading of 'The Mediterranean,'" *University of Kansas City Review* 27 (December 1960): p. 155–9.

Nettels, Elsa. "Aeneas at Washington and The Professor's House: Cather and the Southern Agrarians," in *Willa Cather's Southern Connections: New Essays on Cather and the South* (Charlottesville: Virginia University Press, 2000): p. 170–9.

O'Gorman, Farrell. "The Angelic Artist in the Fiction of Flannery O'Connor and Walker Percy," *Renascence* 53:1 (Fall 2000): p. 61–79.

Pinsker, Sanford. "Why Literary Types (Often) Maintain Friendships that (Some) Public Intellectuals Can't," *The Georgia Review* 53:3 (Fall 1999): p. 591–600.

Pratt, William, ed., *The Fugitive Poets: Modern Southern Poetry in Perspective*, New York: Dutton, 1965.

Pritchard, John Paul, *Criticism in America*, Norman: University of Oklahoma Press, 1956.

Prunty, Wyatt. "At Home and Abroad: Southern Poets with Passports and Memory," *Southern Review* 30:4 (1994): p. 745–50.

Purdy, Rob Roy, ed. *Fugitives Reunion: Conversations at Vanderbilt*, Nashville: Vanderbilt University Press, 1959.

Ransom, John Crowe, ed. *The Kenyon Critics*, New York: World, 1951.

Rubin, Louis. "The Gathering of the Fugitives: A Recollection," *The Southern Review* 30 (Autumn 1994): p. 658–73.

———. and R.D. Jacobs, eds. *South: Modern Southern Literature in Its Cultural Setting*, New York: Doubleday, 1961.

Simpson, Lewis P. "Allen Tate," *The Sewanee Review* 94 (Summer 1986): p. 471–85.

Spears, Monroe K., *Dionysus and the City: Modernism in Twentieth-Century Poetry*, New York: Oxford University Press, 1970.

Squires, Radcliffe. *Allen Tate: A Literary Biography*. New York: Pegasus, 1971.

———. ed., *Allen Tate and His Work: Critical Evaluations*, Minneapolis: University of Minnesota Press, 1972.

Stewart, John L. *The Burden of Time: The Fugitives and Agrarians:*

The Nashville Groups of the 1920's and 1930's, and the Writing of John Crowe Ransom, Allen Tate, and Robert Penn Warren. Princeton: Princeton University Press, 1965.

Stineback, David C., *Shifting World: Social Change and Nostalgia in the American Novel,* Associated University Presses, 1976.

Sullivan, Walter. "Another Southern Connection: Allen Tate and Peter Taylor," *The Sewanee Review* 110:3 (Summer 2002): p. 465–71.

———. *Allen Tate: A Recollection.* Baton Rouge: Louisiana State University Press, 1988.

Tate, Allen; Emily S. Bingham and Thomas A. Underwood. "The Problem of the Unemployed: A Modest Proposal." *New England Review* 22:3 (Summer 2001): p. 153–64.

Tipton, Nathan G. "Queer Be Dragons: Homosocial Identity and Homoerotic Poetics in Robert Penn Warren's 'Brother To Dragons'," *The Mississippi Quarterly* 55:2 (Spring 2002): p. 231-45.

Underwood, Thomas A. *Allen Tate: Orphan of the South.* Princeton: Princeton University Press, 2000.

Vinh, Alphonse, ed. *Cleanth Brooks and Allen Tate: Collected Letters, 1933–1976,* Columbia: University of Missouri Press (Columbia, MO), 1998.

Weingart, S.L. "Cold Revery: Remembering Allen Tate," *The Sewanee Review* 103 (Spring 1995): p. 281–7.

West, Thomas R., *Nature, Community, & Will: A Study in Literary and Social Thought,* Columbia: University of Missouri Press, 1976.

Young, Thomas Daniel and John J. Hindle, eds. *The Republic of Letters in America: The Correspondence of John Peale Bishop and Allen Tate,* Lexington: University Press of Kentucky, 1981.

———. and Elizabeth Sarcone, eds. *The Lytle/Tate Letters, with Allen Tate,* Jackson: University Press of Mississippi, 1987.

ACKNOWLEDGMENTS

Allen Tate by George Hemphill. © 1964 by University of Minnesota Press. Reprinted by permission.

Allen Tate by Ferman Bishop. © 1967 by Twayne Publishers. Reprinted by permission of the Gale Group.

Allen Tate: A Literary Biography by Radcliffe Squires. © 1971 by the Bobbs-Merrill Company, Inc. Reprinted by permission.

Allen Tate and the Augustinian Imagination: A Study of Poetry by Robert S. Dupree. © 1983 by Louisiana State University Press. Reprinted by permission.

The Years of Our Friendship: Robert Lowell and Allen Tate by William Doreski. © 1990 by the University Press of Mississippi. Reprinted by permission.

Hart Crane & Allen Tate: Janus-Faced Modernism by Langdon Hammer. © 1993 by Princeton University Press. Reprinted with permission of The Princeton University Press.

"Aeneas and *The Professor's House*" by Elsa Nettels. From *Willa Cather's Southern Connections: New Essays on Cather and the South*. Ed. Ann Romines. © 2000 by The Rector and Visitors of the University of Virginia. Reprinted by permission.

Allen Tate: Orphan of the South by Thomas A. Underwood. © 2000 by Thomas Andrew Underwood. Reprinted with permission of the Princeton University Press.

INDEX OF

Themes and Ideas

"AENEAS AT WASHINGTON," critical analysis of, 78–81; critical views of, 9, 11, 68, 70, 82–91; critique of the city in, 84–87; memory in, 88–91; theme of, 82–83

"AMBITIOUS NOVEMBER," 49

"ATLANTIS," 59

"BURIED LAKE, THE," 60, 82–83, 103

"CAUSERIE," 54, 68

COLLECTED POEMS, 59, 78, 115

"CRANE: THE POET AS HERO," 59

"DEATH OF LITTLE BOYS," 83

DOUBLE DEALER, THE, 40

"DREAM, A," 66–67

"EAGLE, THE," 66

"ELEGY," 66

ESSAYS OF FOUR DECADES, 58, 61

"FRAGMENT OF A MEDITATION," 68

"IGNIS FATUUS," 44, 66

"LAST DAYS OF ALICE," 67

"MAIMED MAN, THE," 60, 82, 97–99, 102–3

"MEANING OF DEATH, THE," 67

"MEDITERRANEAN, THE," alternating tension and relaxation in, 66–68; Baudelaire's influence in, 75–77; critical analysis of, 63–65; critical views of, 9–11, 65–78, 82, 84, 113; Greek and Roman imitation in, 71–74; sense of myth in, 68–71

"MR. POPE," 54

"NARCISSUS AS NARCISSUS," 30, 41, 46, 50, 59–61

"ODE TO FEAR," 66

"ODE: TO OUR YOUNG PROCONSULS OF THE AIR," 72

"ODE TO THE CONFEDERATE DEAD," critical analysis of, 18–24; critical views of, 9–10, 25–62, 71, 78, 82–83, 86; intent and technique of, 29–46; language in, 53–55; social ideas in, 25–29; speaker's crisis in, 47–53

"ON A PORTRAIT OF HART CRANE," 40

"PARADIGM, THE," 66

"PICNIC AT CASSIS," 71

"PROFESSION OF LETTERS IN THE SOUTH, THE," 75

"RETRODUCTION TO AMERICAN HISTORY," 68

"SEASONS OF THE SOUL," 82

SONNETS AT CHRISTMAS, 99, 107, 113

"SUBWAY, THE," 47, 54, 67

"SWIMMERS, THE," critical analysis of, 92–95; critical views of, 9, 60, 82–83, 96–112; formal approach of, 96–97; narrative of, 97–102; segregation and integration in, 106–12; symbolism in, 97–102; use of child personae in, 102–6

TATE, ALLEN, Baudelaire's influence on, 9, 75–77; biography of, 12–17; Eliot and Crane's impact on, 9–11, 33, 55–62; imaginative vision of, 9; language of, 53–55; social ideas of, 25–29; works about, 116–20; works by 113–15

"TEETH," 43

"TENSION IN POETRY," 66–67

"THESE DEATHY LEAVES," 43

"TRANSLATION OR IMITATIONS," 77

"WINTER MASK," 82